BIRDHOUSES, FEEDERS
You can make

by

Hi Sibley

South Holland, Illinois
THE GOODHEART-WILLCOX COMPANY, INC.
Publishers

ATTRACTING BIRDS TO YOUR LAWN AND GARDEN
MATERIALS SUGGESTED

(Read Before Starting Construction)

It has been demonstrated that the total bird population in a given area can be raised far above normal by supplying nesting boxes and feeders. Species of birds that may be attracted include:

Bluebird	Starling
Robin	Phoebe
Chickadee	Crested Flycatcher
Titmouse	Flicker
Nuthatch	Golden-Fronted Woodpecker
House Wren	Redheaded Woodpecker
Carolina Wren	Downy Woodpecker
Violet Green Swallow	Hairy Woodpecker
Tree Swallow	Screech Owl
Barn Swallow	Saw-Whet Owl
Purple Martin	Barn Owl
Song Sparrow	Sparrow Hawk
House Finch	Wood Duck

Materials well suited for use in building bird houses and feeders are 1/4, 3/8, and 1/2 in. exterior plywood; 1/2 and 3/4 in. solid cypress, redwood, red cedar, white pine, and yellow poplar.

The thickness of materials generally used for end, side, and roof pieces are 1/4, 3/8, and 1/2; and 1/2 and 3/4 in. materials are commonly used for the floors.

In building hopper-type feeders, there should be 1/4 in. clearance between the bottom of the hopper and the floor. When using glass panes, it is a good idea to make saw cuts to accept the glass, and to place a brad about 1/4 in. from the bottom of the saw cut to serve as a stop.

Where drawings specify a particular type of material, other materials can usually be substituted, if slight modifications are made in the dimensions and construction procedure.

Paint is not objectionable to birds if soft tones of brown, gray, or dull green are used.

Roofs should be made with sufficient pitch to provide good drainage. If the design requires that the roof be nearly level, a groove should be cut across the overhang on the underside to prevent water from draining back into the interior of the house. The overhang should be a minimum of 2 in. to prevent water from going into the entrance hole during a driving rain. In freezing latitudes the sides should extend below the floor of the box, thus draining off water that might otherwise freeze in the joint and wedge it apart. It is a good idea to drill a few 1/8 in. holes in the floor to drain away any water or melted snow that gets into the house.

For bird house ventilation, three or four 1/4 in. holes may be drilled in the side near the entrance, just under the roof. An exception is for Martin houses. A draft would ensue because the entrance is near the floor. For Martin houses a single 1/4 in. vent should be drilled near the top.

Library of Congress Catalog Card Number 90-24053
International Standard Book Number 0-87006-843-1

234567890-91-98765432

Library of Congress Cataloging in Publication Data

Sibley, Hi
  Bird houses, feeders you can make / by Hi Sibley
      p. cm.
    Rev. ed. of: 102 bird houses, feeders you can make. c1976.
    ISBN 0-87006-843-1
    1. Birdhouses—Design and construction.
  2. Bird feeders—Design and construction.
  I. Sibley, Hi, 102 bird houses, feeders you can make.
  II. Title.
  QL676.5.S46   1991
  690'.89--dc20   90-24053
                                          CIP

DIMENSIONS OF NESTING BOXES

Species	Floor of cavity	Depth of cavity	Entrance above floor	Dia. of entrance	Height above ground
	Inches	Inches	Inches	Inches	Feet
Bluebird	5x5	8	6	1 1/2	5 — 10
Robin	6x8	8	A		6 — 15
Chickadee	4x4	8 — 10	6 — 8	1 1/8	6 — 15
Titmouse	4x4	8 — 10	6 — 8	1 1/4	6 — 15
Nuthatch	4x4	8 — 10	6 — 8	1 1/4	12 — 20
House Wren	4x4	6 — 8	1 — 6	1 1/4	6 — 10
Carolina Wren	4x4	6 — 8	1 — 6	1 1/2	6 — 10
Violet Green Swallow	5x5	6	1 — 5	1 1/2	10 — 15
Tree Swallow	5x5	6	1 — 5	1 1/2	10 — 15
Barn Swallow	6x6	6	B	B	8 — 12
Purple Martin	6x6	6	1	2 1/2	15 — 20
Song Sparrow	6x6	6	B	B	1 — 3
House Finch	6x6	6	4	2	8 — 12
Starling	6x6	16 — 18	14 — 16	2	10 — 25
Phoebe	6x6	6	A	A	8 — 12
Crested Flycatcher	6x6	8 — 10	6 — 8	2	8 — 20
Flicker	7x7	16 — 18	14 — 16	2 1/2	6 — 20
Golden-Fronted Woodpecker	6x6	12 — 15	9 — 12	2	12 — 20
Redheaded Woodpecker	6x6	12 — 15	9 — 12	2	12 — 20
Downy Woodpecker	4x4	8 — 10	6 — 8	1 1/4	6 — 20
Hairy Woodpecker	6x6	12 — 15	9 — 12	1 1/2	12 — 20
Screech Owl	8x8	12 — 15	9 — 12	3	10 — 30
Saw-Whet Owl	6x6	10 — 12	8 — 10	2 1/2	12 — 20
Barn Owl	10 — 18	15 — 18	4	6	12 — 18
Sparrow Hawk	8x8	12 — 15	9 — 12	3	10 — 30
Wood Duck	10 — 18	10 — 24	12 — 16	4	10 — 20

A — one or more sides open.   B — all sides open.

LOG CABIN BIRDHOUSE

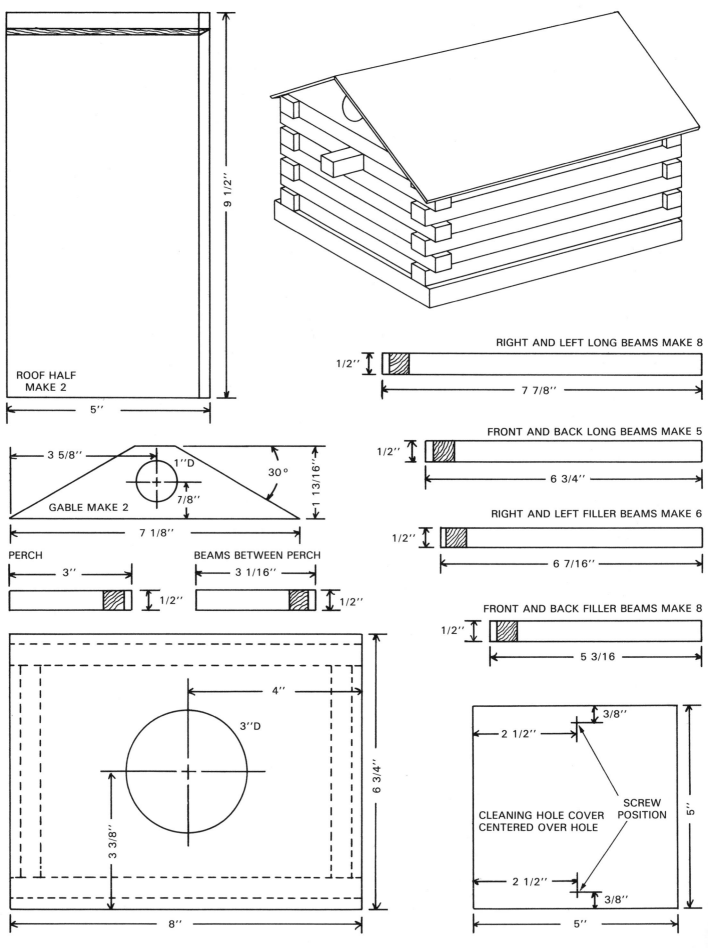

ROOF HALF
MAKE 2

9 1/2"

5"

RIGHT AND LEFT LONG BEAMS MAKE 8

1/2"

7 7/8"

FRONT AND BACK LONG BEAMS MAKE 5

1/2"

6 3/4"

3 5/8"   1"D   30°   1 13/16"

GABLE MAKE 2   7/8"

7 1/8"

RIGHT AND LEFT FILLER BEAMS MAKE 6

1/2"

6 7/16"

PERCH   BEAMS BETWEEN PERCH

3"   3 1/16"

1/2"   1/2"

FRONT AND BACK FILLER BEAMS MAKE 8

1/2"

5 3/16

4"   3"D   6 3/4"

3 3/8"

8"

3/8"

2 1/2"

CLEANING HOLE COVER
CENTERED OVER HOLE   SCREW
POSITION

5"

2 1/2"

3/8"

5"

FOR BLUEBIRD AND TREE SWALLOW

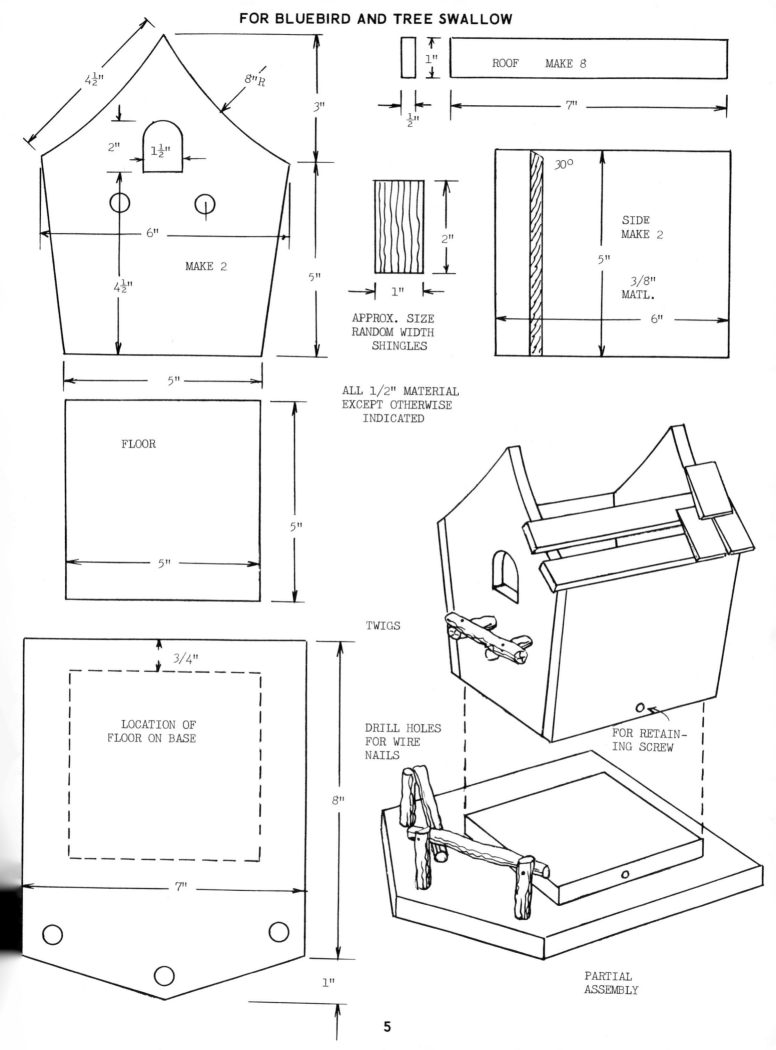

4½"

8"R

3"

2" 1½"

6"

MAKE 2

4½"

5"

5"

FLOOR

5"

5"

3/4"

LOCATION OF
FLOOR ON BASE

8"

7"

1"

ROOF   MAKE 8

1"

½"

7"

2"

1"

APPROX. SIZE
RANDOM WIDTH
SHINGLES

ALL 1/2" MATERIAL
EXCEPT OTHERWISE
INDICATED

30°

SIDE
MAKE 2

5"

3/8"
MATL.

6"

TWIGS

DRILL HOLES
FOR WIRE
NAILS

FOR RETAIN-
ING SCREW

PARTIAL
ASSEMBLY

5

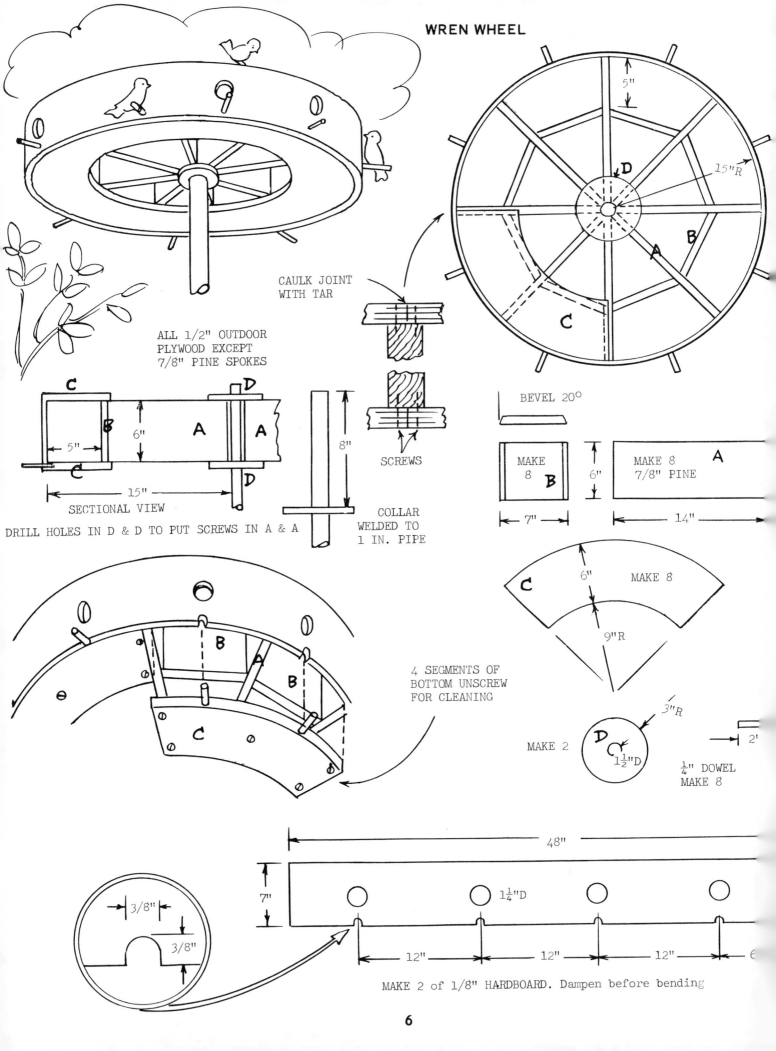

WREN WHEEL

5"

15"R

D

B

A

C

CAULK JOINT
WITH TAR

ALL 1/2" OUTDOOR
PLYWOOD EXCEPT
7/8" PINE SPOKES

C

D

B

A   A

D

C

6"

5"

15"

SECTIONAL VIEW

DRILL HOLES IN D & D TO PUT SCREWS IN A & A

8"

COLLAR
WELDED TO
1 IN. PIPE

SCREWS

BEVEL 20°

MAKE
8   B

MAKE 8
7/8" PINE   A

6"

7"

14"

C

6"

MAKE 8

9"R

4 SEGMENTS OF
BOTTOM UNSCREW
FOR CLEANING

B

B

A

C

MAKE 2   D

1½"D   3"R

¼" DOWEL
MAKE 8   2'

48"

7"

1¼"D

12"   12"   12"

3/8"

3/8"

MAKE 2 of 1/8" HARDBOARD. Dampen before bending

6

MEETING HOUSE for MARTINS

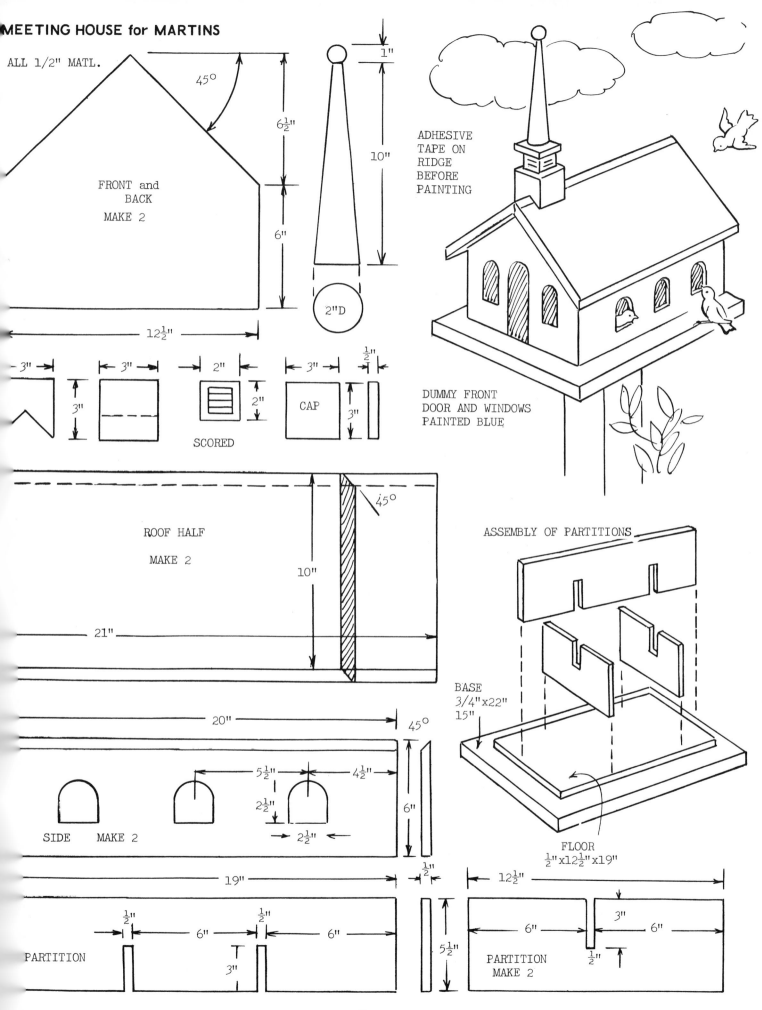

ALL 1/2" MATL.

45°

FRONT and
BACK
MAKE 2

6½"

6"

12½"

1"

10"

2"D

ADHESIVE
TAPE ON
RIDGE
BEFORE
PAINTING

3"   3"   2"   3"   ½"

3"   2"   CAP   3"

SCORED

DUMMY FRONT
DOOR AND WINDOWS
PAINTED BLUE

ROOF HALF

MAKE 2

45°

10"

21"

20"   45°

5½"   4½"

2½"

6"

2½"

SIDE   MAKE 2

19"   ½"

½"   6"   ½"   6"

PARTITION   3"

ASSEMBLY OF PARTITIONS

BASE
3/4"x22"
15"

FLOOR
½"x12½"x19"

12½"

6"   3"   6"

5½"   ½"

PARTITION
MAKE 2

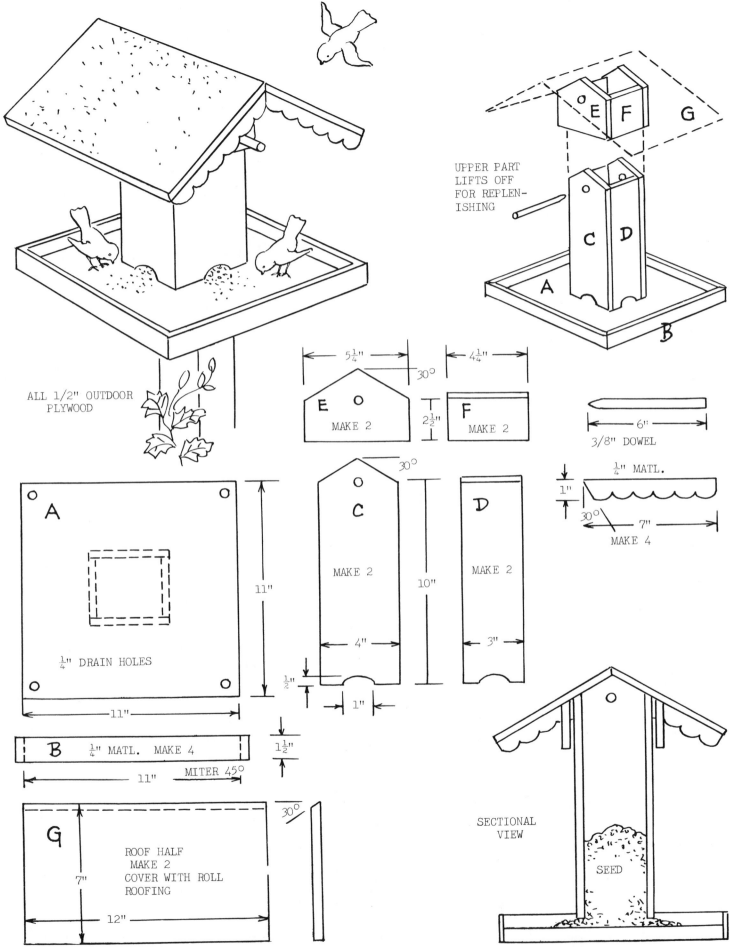

SWISS FEEDER

UPPER PART
LIFTS OFF
FOR REPLEN-
ISHING

ALL 1/2" OUTDOOR
PLYWOOD

5¼"   4¼"
30°

E O
MAKE 2

2½"

F
MAKE 2

6"
3/8" DOWEL

30°

C
MAKE 2

10"

4"

½"

1"

D
MAKE 2

3"

¼" MATL.
1"
30°   7"
MAKE 4

A

¼" DRAIN HOLES

11"

11"

B   ¼" MATL.   MAKE 4

1½"

11"   MITER 45°

G
ROOF HALF
MAKE 2
COVER WITH ROLL
ROOFING

30°

7"

12"

SECTIONAL
VIEW

SEED

FOUR-APARTMENT FOR WRENS

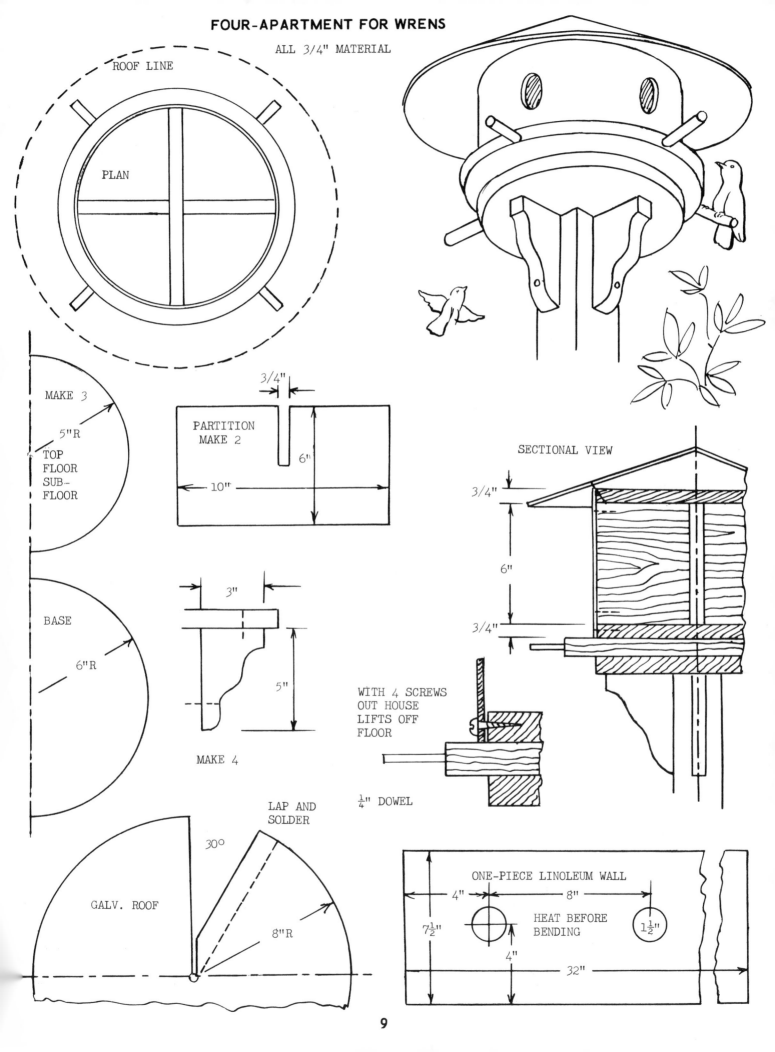

ALL 3/4" MATERIAL

ROOF LINE

PLAN

MAKE 3

5"R

TOP
FLOOR
SUB-
FLOOR

BASE

6"R

3/4"

PARTITION
MAKE 2

10"

6"

3"

5"

MAKE 4

LAP AND
SOLDER

30°

GALV. ROOF

8"R

SECTIONAL VIEW

3/4"

6"

3/4"

WITH 4 SCREWS
OUT HOUSE
LIFTS OFF
FLOOR

¼" DOWEL

ONE-PIECE LINOLEUM WALL

4"

8"

HEAT BEFORE
BENDING

1½"

7½"

4"

32"

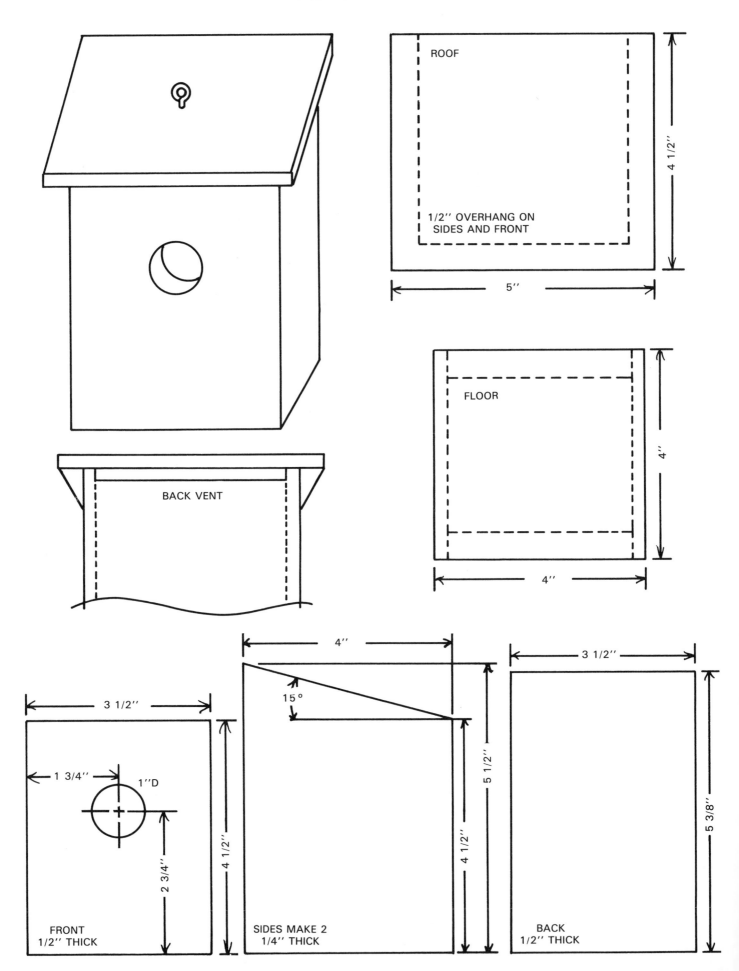

ROOF

1/2'' OVERHANG ON SIDES AND FRONT

4 1/2''

5''

FLOOR

4''

4''

BACK VENT

4''

15°

5 1/2''

4 1/2''

3 1/2''

5 3/8''

3 1/2''

1 3/4''

1''D

2 3/4''

4 1/2''

FRONT
1/2'' THICK

SIDES MAKE 2
1/4'' THICK

BACK
1/2'' THICK

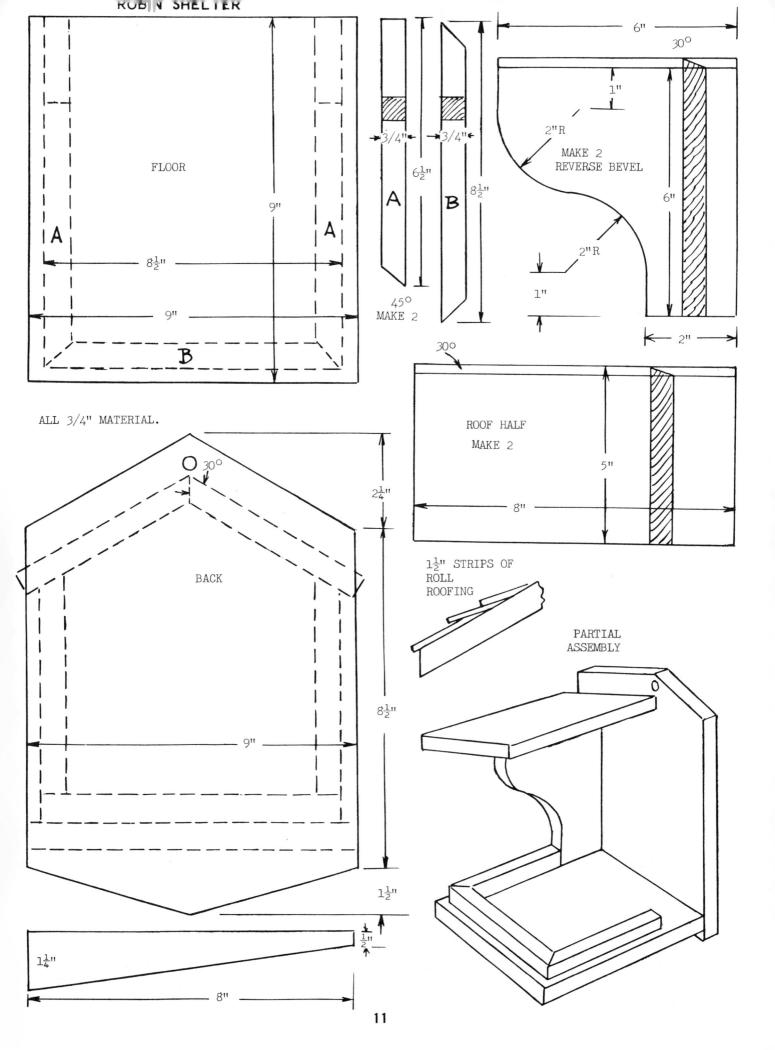

FLOOR

9"

8½"

9"

A A

A

B

45°
MAKE 2

3/4" 3/4"

6½"

8½"

A B

ALL 3/4" MATERIAL.

6"

30°

1"

2"R

MAKE 2
REVERSE BEVEL

2"R

1"

6"

2"

30°

ROOF HALF
MAKE 2

5"

8"

1½" STRIPS OF
ROLL
ROOFING

PARTIAL
ASSEMBLY

O 30°

BACK

2¼"

9"

8½"

1½"

½"

1¼"

8"

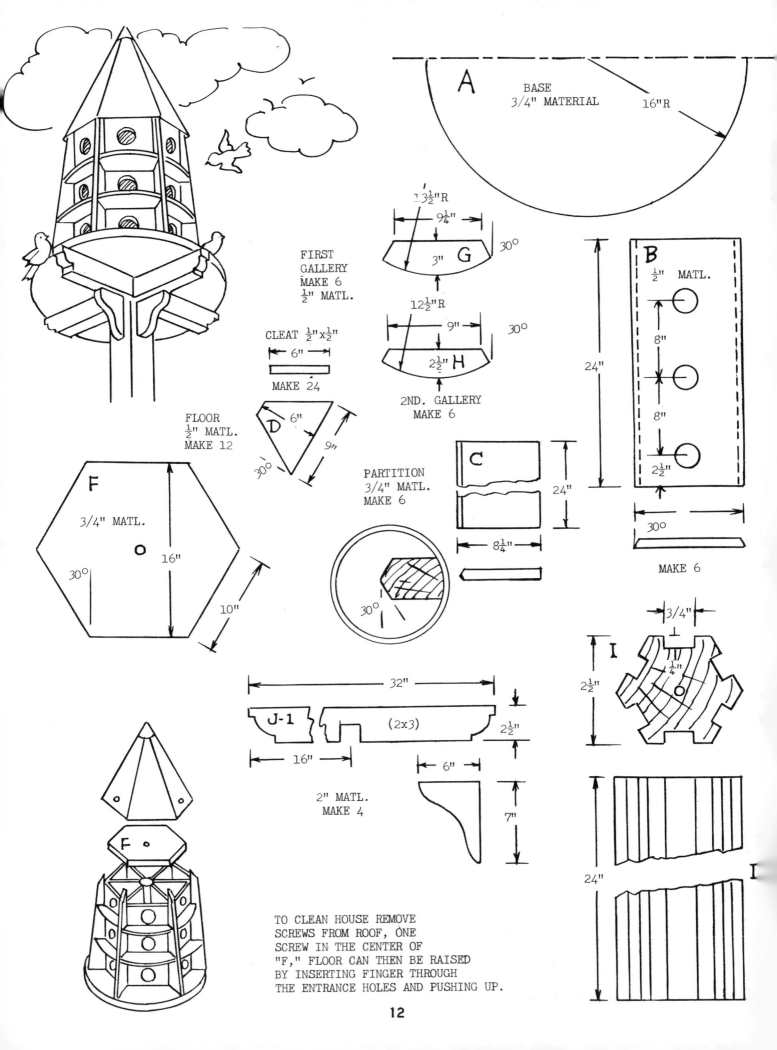

A
BASE
3/4" MATERIAL
16"R

FIRST
GALLERY
MAKE 6
1/2" MATL.

13 1/2"R
9 1/4"
3"   G
30°

CLEAT 1/2"x1/2"
6"
MAKE 24

12 1/2"R
9"
2 1/2"   H
30°

2ND. GALLERY
MAKE 6

FLOOR
1/2" MATL.
MAKE 12

D   6"
9"
30°

PARTITION
3/4" MATL.
MAKE 6

C
24"
8 1/4"

30°

F
3/4" MATL.
o
16"
30°
10"

B
1/2"   MATL.
8"
8"
2 1/2"
24"
30°
MAKE 6

3/4"
I
1/4"
2 1/2"

32"
J-1   (2x3)
2 1/2"
16"
6"
7"

2" MATL.
MAKE 4

24"   I

TO CLEAN HOUSE REMOVE
SCREWS FROM ROOF, ONE
SCREW IN THE CENTER OF
"F," FLOOR CAN THEN BE RAISED
BY INSERTING FINGER THROUGH
THE ENTRANCE HOLES AND PUSHING UP.

F

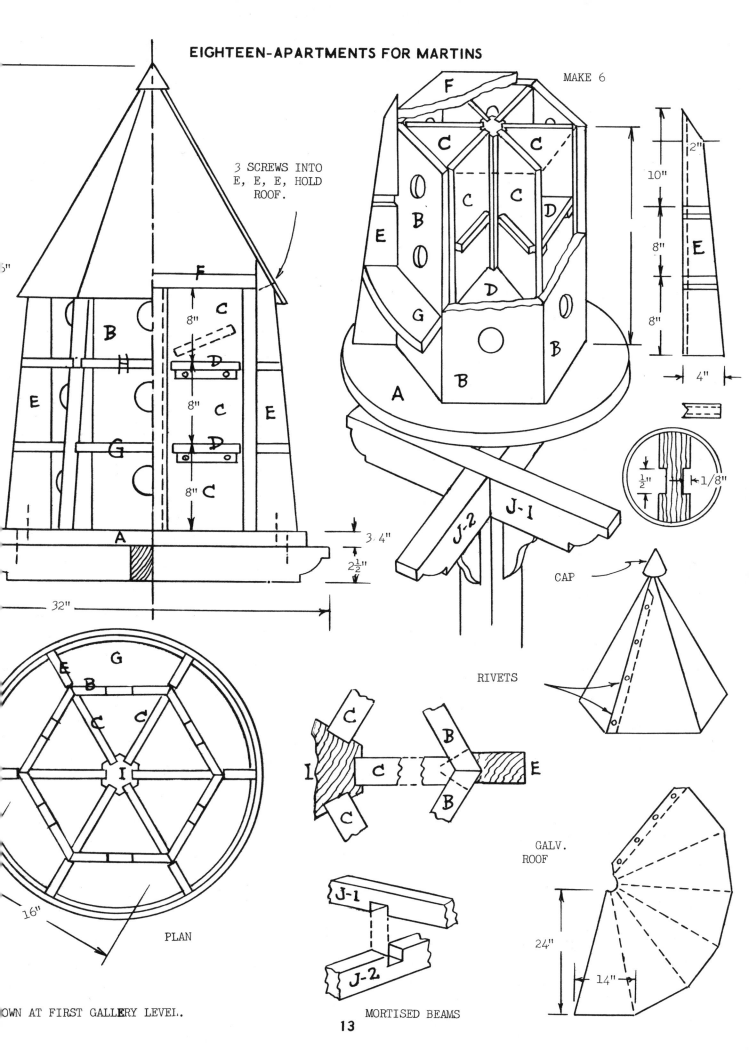

MAKE 6

3 SCREWS INTO
E, E, E, HOLD
ROOF.

8"

8"

8"

3, 4"

2½"

32"

16"

PLAN

OWN AT FIRST GALLERY LEVEL.

2"

10"

8"

8"

4"

½"

1/8"

J-2

J-1

CAP

RIVETS

GALV.
ROOF

24"

14"

J-1

J-2

MORTISED BEAMS

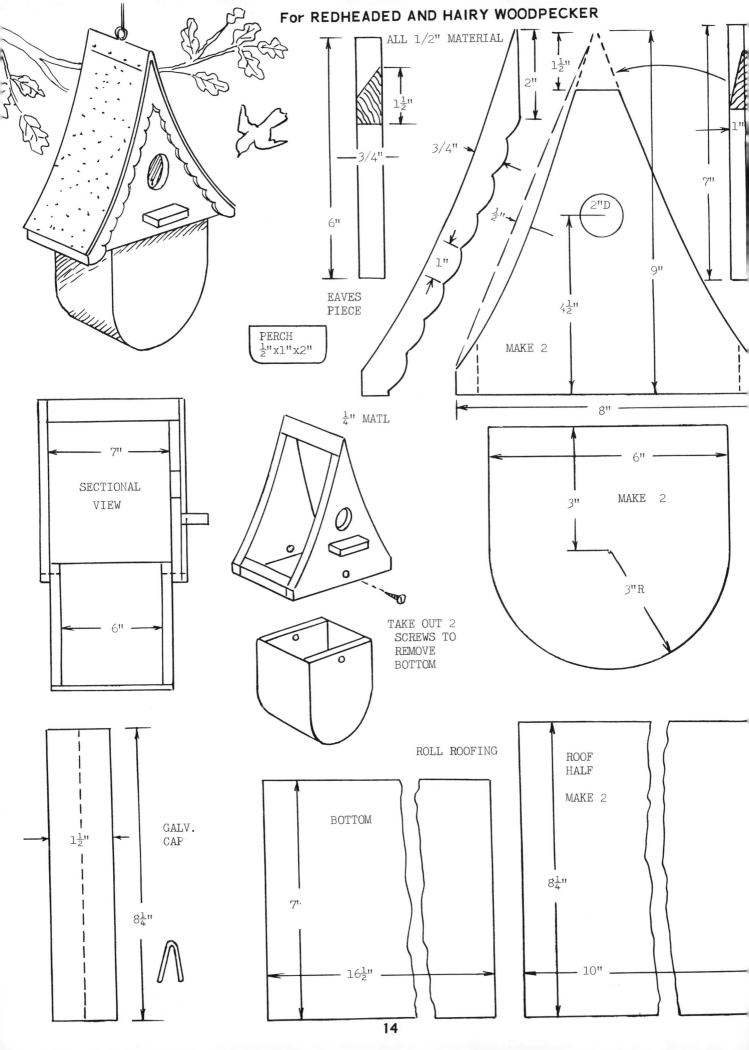

For REDHEADED AND HAIRY WOODPECKER

ALL 1/2" MATERIAL

1½"

3/4"

6"

EAVES
PIECE

PERCH
½"x1"x2"

3/4"

½"

1"

2"

1½"

2"D

4½"

9"

7"

1"

MAKE 2

8"

6"

3"

MAKE 2

3"R

SECTIONAL
VIEW

7"

6"

¼" MATL

TAKE OUT 2
SCREWS TO
REMOVE
BOTTOM

ROLL ROOFING

ROOF
HALF

MAKE 2

8¼"

10"

GALV.
CAP

1½"

8¼"

BOTTOM

7"

16½"

14

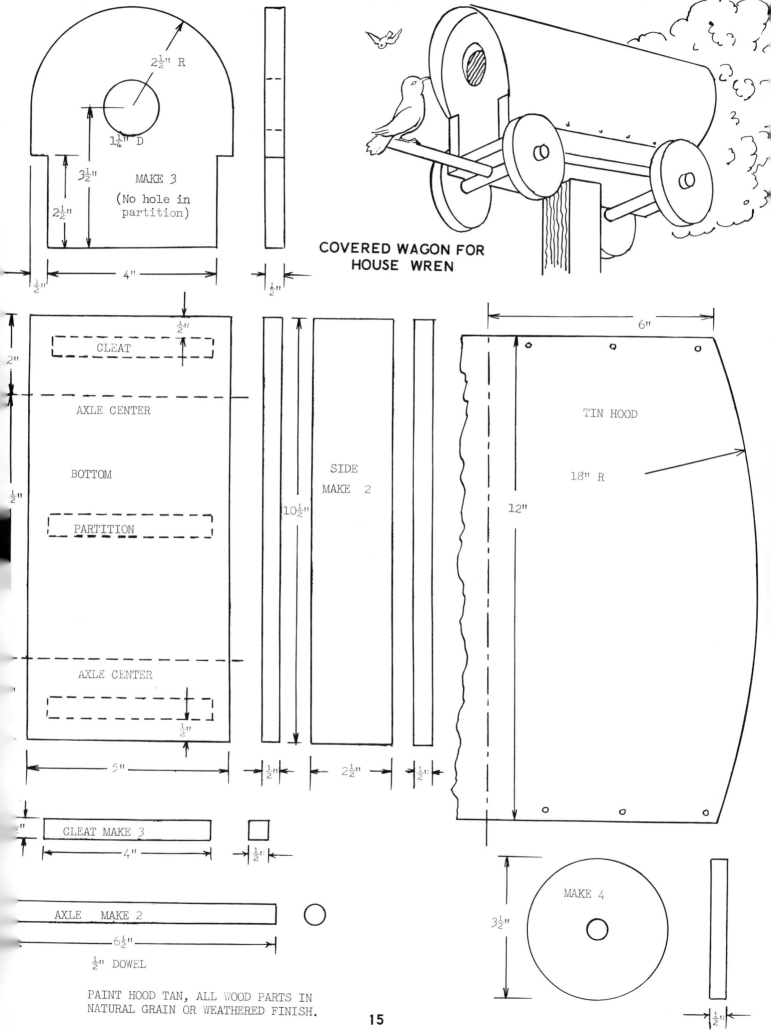

2½" R

1¼" D

3½"

2½"

MAKE 3
(No hole in
partition)

½"

4"

½"

½"

COVERED WAGON FOR
HOUSE WREN

½"

2"

CLEAT

AXLE CENTER

BOTTOM

½"

PARTITION

AXLE CENTER

½"

5"

SIDE
MAKE 2

10½"

½"   2½"   ½"

6"

TIN HOOD

18" R

12"

CLEAT MAKE 3

4"

½"

AXLE   MAKE 2

6½"

½" DOWEL

MAKE 4

3½"

½"

PAINT HOOD TAN, ALL WOOD PARTS IN
NATURAL GRAIN OR WEATHERED FINISH.

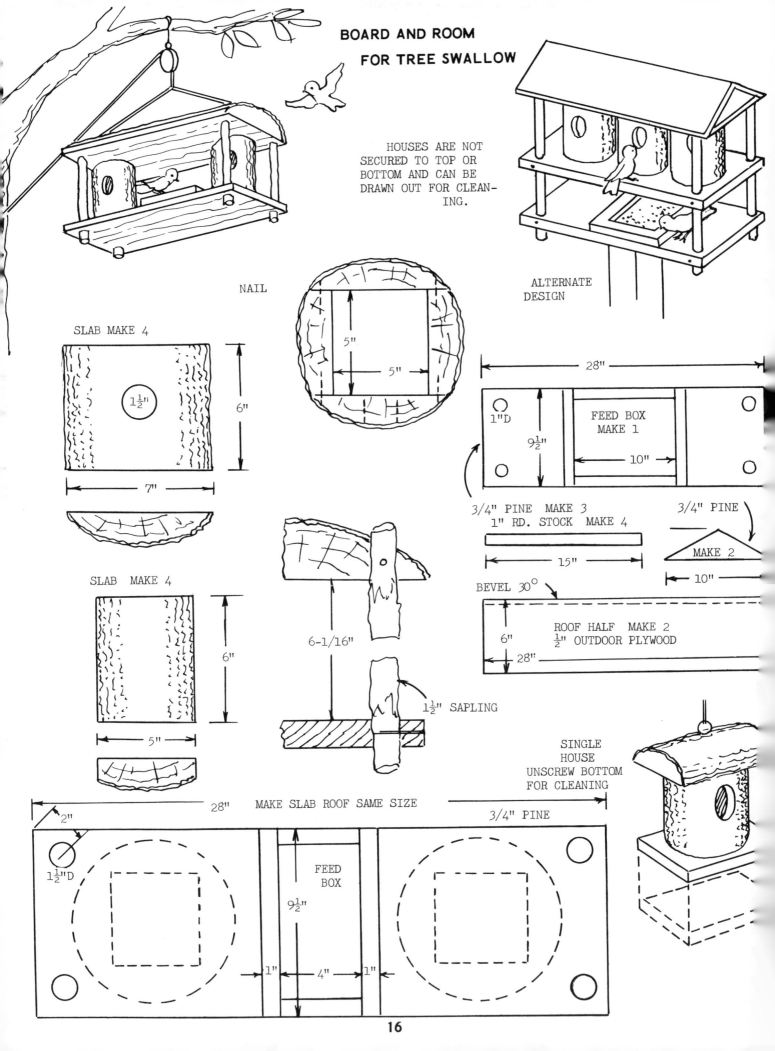

BOARD AND ROOM
FOR TREE SWALLOW

HOUSES ARE NOT
SECURED TO TOP OR
BOTTOM AND CAN BE
DRAWN OUT FOR CLEAN-
ING.

NAIL

ALTERNATE
DESIGN

SLAB MAKE 4

$1\frac{1}{2}$"

6"

7"

5"

5"

28"

1"D

FEED BOX
MAKE 1

$9\frac{1}{2}$"

10"

3/4" PINE   MAKE 3
1" RD. STOCK   MAKE 4

3/4" PINE

MAKE 2

15"

10"

SLAB   MAKE 4

6"

5"

6-1/16"

$1\frac{1}{2}$" SAPLING

BEVEL 30°

ROOF HALF   MAKE 2
$\frac{1}{2}$" OUTDOOR PLYWOOD

6"

28"

SINGLE
HOUSE
UNSCREW BOTTOM
FOR CLEANING

28"   MAKE SLAB ROOF SAME SIZE   3/4" PINE

2"

$1\frac{1}{2}$"D

FEED
BOX

$9\frac{1}{2}$"

1"   4"   1"

16

PUEBLO FOR HOUSE FINCH

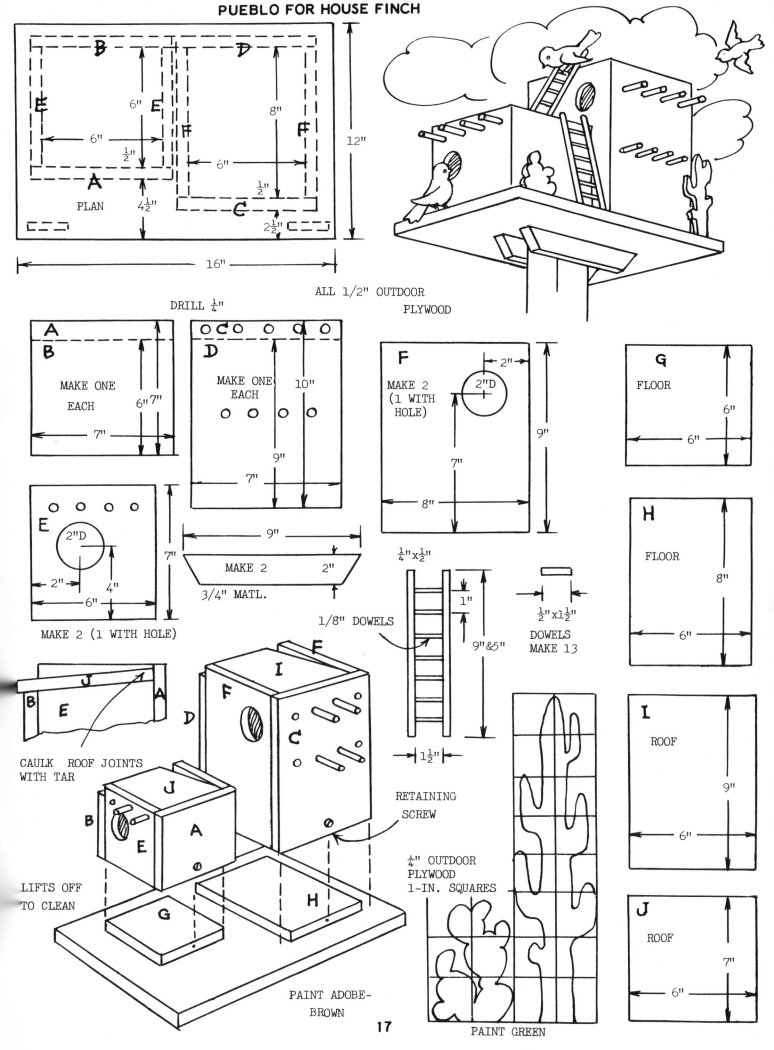

PLAN

12"

16"

6"

6"

8"

6"

4½"

2½"

½"

½"

DRILL ¼"

ALL 1/2" OUTDOOR PLYWOOD

A
B

MAKE ONE EACH

6" 7"

7"

C
D

MAKE ONE EACH

10"

9"

7"

F

MAKE 2 (1 WITH HOLE)

2"

2"D

7"

9"

8"

G

FLOOR

6"

6"

H

FLOOR

8"

6"

E

2"D

2"

4"

6"

7"

MAKE 2 (1 WITH HOLE)

9"

2"

MAKE 2

3/4" MATL.

1/8" DOWELS

¼" x ½"

1"

9" & 5"

1½"

½" x 1½"

DOWELS
MAKE 13

I

ROOF

9"

6"

CAULK ROOF JOINTS WITH TAR

RETAINING SCREW

LIFTS OFF TO CLEAN

PAINT ADOBE-BROWN

¼" OUTDOOR PLYWOOD
1-IN. SQUARES

PAINT GREEN

J

ROOF

7"

6"

17

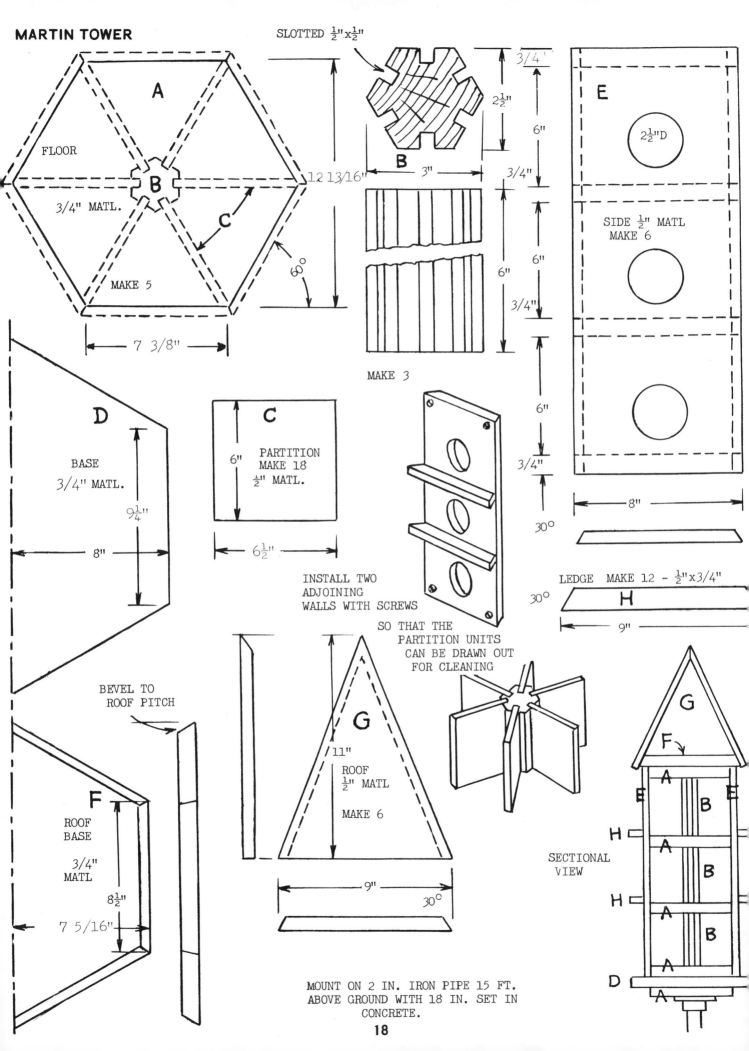

MARTIN TOWER

SLOTTED ½"x½"

A

FLOOR

3/4" MATL.

MAKE 5

12 13/16"

60°

7 3/8"

B

3"

2½"

3/4"

MAKE 3

3/4"

6"

3/4"

6"

3/4"

6"

3/4"

6"

3/4"

30°

30°

E

2½"D

SIDE ½" MATL
MAKE 6

8"

LEDGE   MAKE 12 - ½"x3/4"

H

9"

D

BASE
3/4" MATL.

9¼"

8"

C

6"

PARTITION
MAKE 18
½" MATL.

6½"

INSTALL TWO
ADJOINING
WALLS WITH SCREWS

SO THAT THE
PARTITION UNITS
CAN BE DRAWN OUT
FOR CLEANING

BEVEL TO
ROOF PITCH

F

ROOF
BASE

3/4"
MATL

8½"

7 5/16"

G

11"

ROOF
½" MATL

MAKE 6

9"

30°

MOUNT ON 2 IN. IRON PIPE 15 FT.
ABOVE GROUND WITH 18 IN. SET IN
CONCRETE.

G

F

A

E

B

E

H

A

B

H

A

B

A

D

A

SECTIONAL
VIEW

18

HALF-TIMBERED BIRDHOUSE

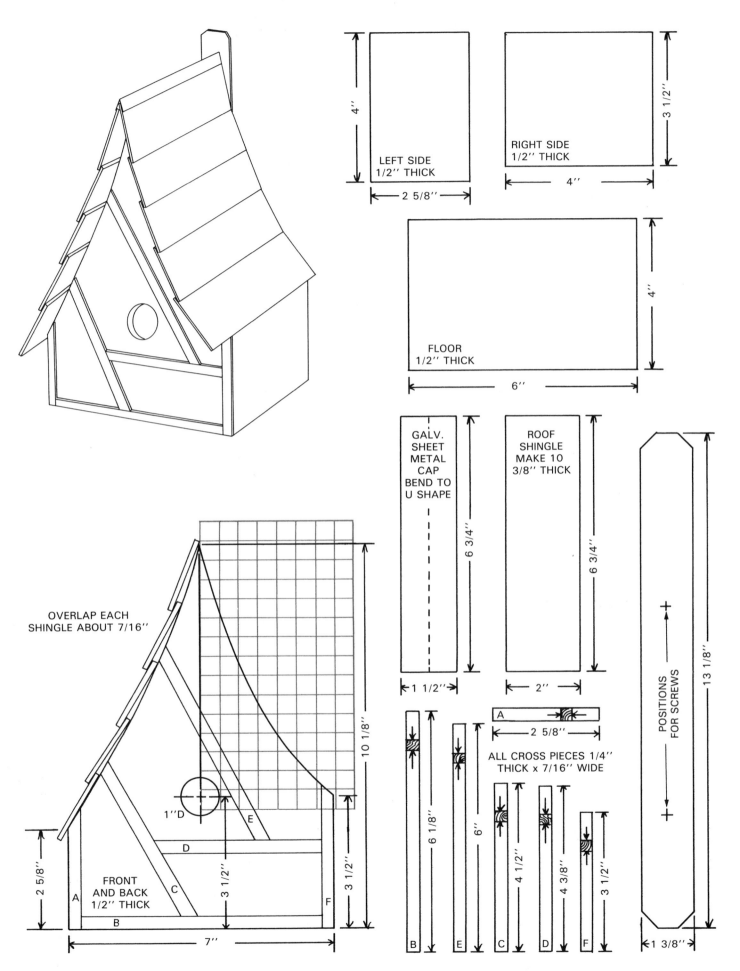

LEFT SIDE
1/2'' THICK

4''

2 5/8''

RIGHT SIDE
1/2'' THICK

3 1/2''

4''

FLOOR
1/2'' THICK

4''

6''

GALV.
SHEET
METAL
CAP
BEND TO
U SHAPE

6 3/4''

1 1/2''

ROOF
SHINGLE
MAKE 10
3/8'' THICK

6 3/4''

2''

A

2 5/8''

ALL CROSS PIECES 1/4''
THICK x 7/16'' WIDE

POSITIONS FOR SCREWS

13 1/8''

1 3/8''

OVERLAP EACH
SHINGLE ABOUT 7/16''

10 1/8''

1''D

E

D

C

3 1/2''

A

FRONT
AND BACK
1/2'' THICK

B

F

2 5/8''

3 1/2''

7''

B

6 1/8''

E

6''

C

4 1/2''

D

4 3/8''

F

3 1/2''

19

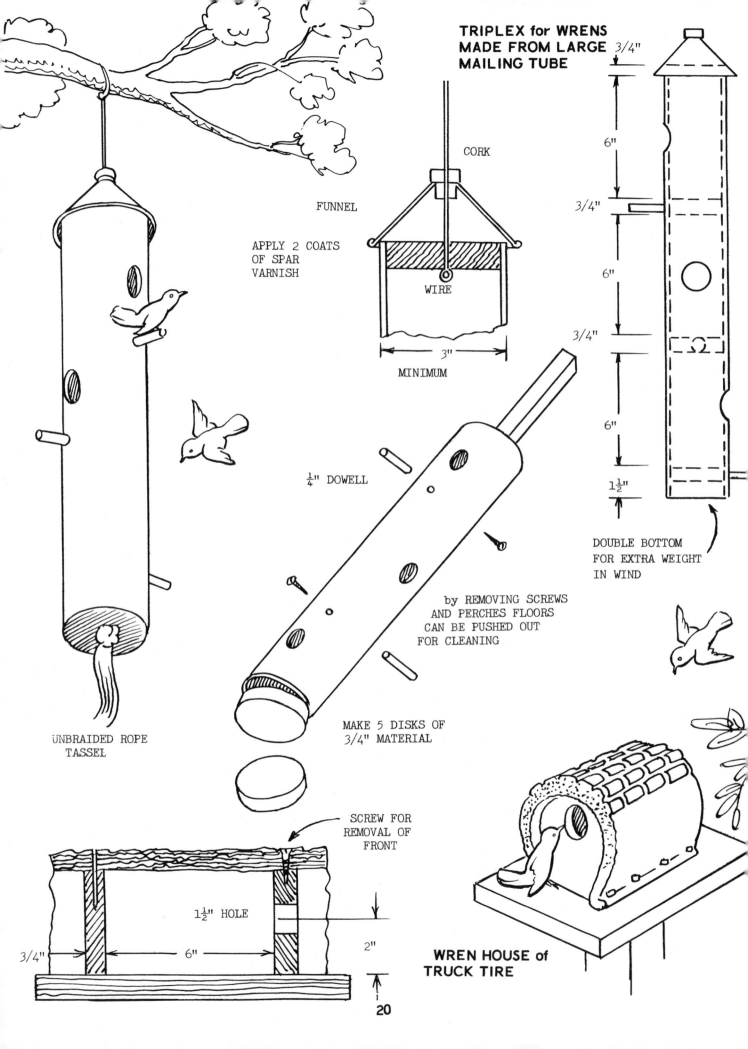

TRIPLEX for WRENS
MADE FROM LARGE
MAILING TUBE

CORK

FUNNEL

APPLY 2 COATS
OF SPAR
VARNISH

WIRE

3"

MINIMUM

3/4"

6"

3/4"

6"

3/4"

6"

1½"

DOUBLE BOTTOM
FOR EXTRA WEIGHT
IN WIND

¼" DOWELL

by REMOVING SCREWS
AND PERCHES FLOORS
CAN BE PUSHED OUT
FOR CLEANING

MAKE 5 DISKS OF
3/4" MATERIAL

UNBRAIDED ROPE
TASSEL

SCREW FOR
REMOVAL OF
FRONT

1½" HOLE

3/4"   6"

2"

WREN HOUSE of
TRUCK TIRE

20

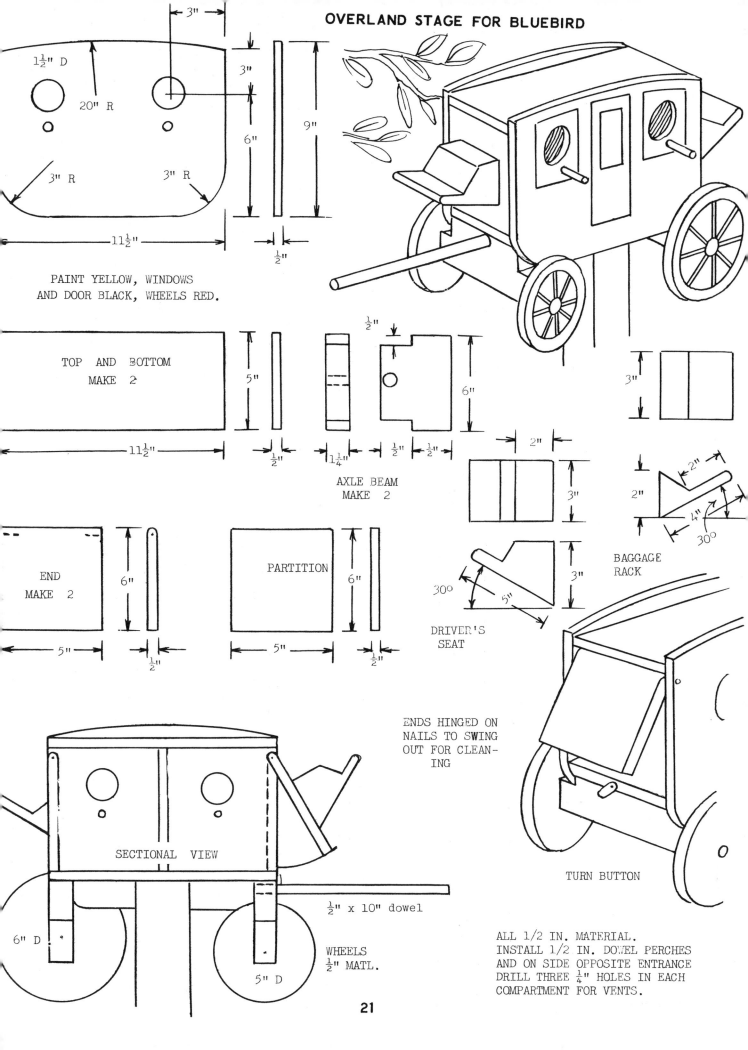

$1\frac{1}{2}$" D

3"

20" R

3"

3"

6"

9"

3" R

3" R

$11\frac{1}{2}$"

$\frac{1}{2}$"

PAINT YELLOW, WINDOWS
AND DOOR BLACK, WHEELS RED.

TOP AND BOTTOM
MAKE 2

5"

$\frac{1}{2}$"

$11\frac{1}{2}$"

$\frac{1}{2}$"

$1\frac{1}{4}$"

$\frac{1}{2}$"

$\frac{1}{2}$"

$\frac{1}{2}$"

6"

AXLE BEAM
MAKE 2

3"

2"

3"

2"

2"

4"

30°

BAGGAGE
RACK

END
MAKE 2

6"

5"

$\frac{1}{2}$"

PARTITION

6"

5"

$\frac{1}{2}$"

30°

5"

3"

DRIVER'S
SEAT

ENDS HINGED ON
NAILS TO SWING
OUT FOR CLEAN-
ING

SECTIONAL VIEW

6" D

5" D

$\frac{1}{2}$" x 10" dowel

WHEELS
$\frac{1}{2}$" MATL.

TURN BUTTON

ALL 1/2 IN. MATERIAL.
INSTALL 1/2 IN. DOWEL PERCHES
AND ON SIDE OPPOSITE ENTRANCE
DRILL THREE $\frac{1}{4}$" HOLES IN EACH
COMPARTMENT FOR VENTS.

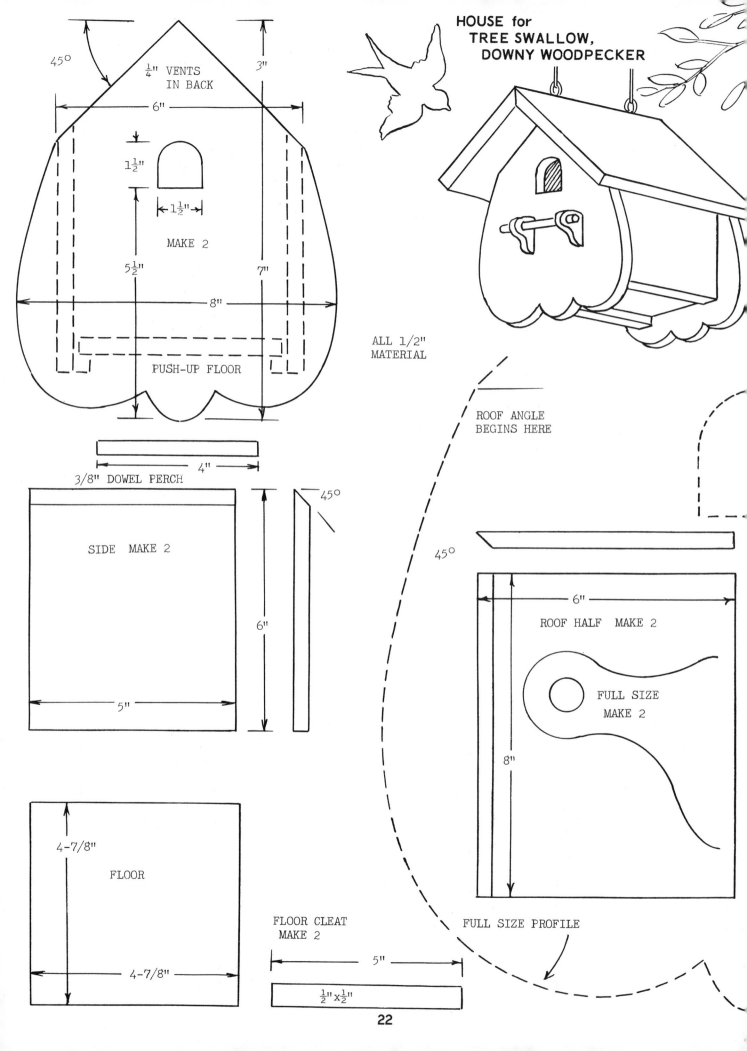

45°

¼" VENTS
IN BACK

3"

6"

1½"

←1½"→

MAKE 2

5½"

7"

8"

PUSH-UP FLOOR

4"

3/8" DOWEL PERCH

SIDE MAKE 2

6"

5"

45°

4-7/8"

FLOOR

4-7/8"

FLOOR CLEAT
MAKE 2

5"

½"x½"

HOUSE for
**TREE SWALLOW,
DOWNY WOODPECKER**

ALL ½"
MATERIAL

ROOF ANGLE
BEGINS HERE

45°

6"

ROOF HALF MAKE 2

FULL SIZE
MAKE 2

8"

FULL SIZE PROFILE

22

TILT-TOP FEEDER

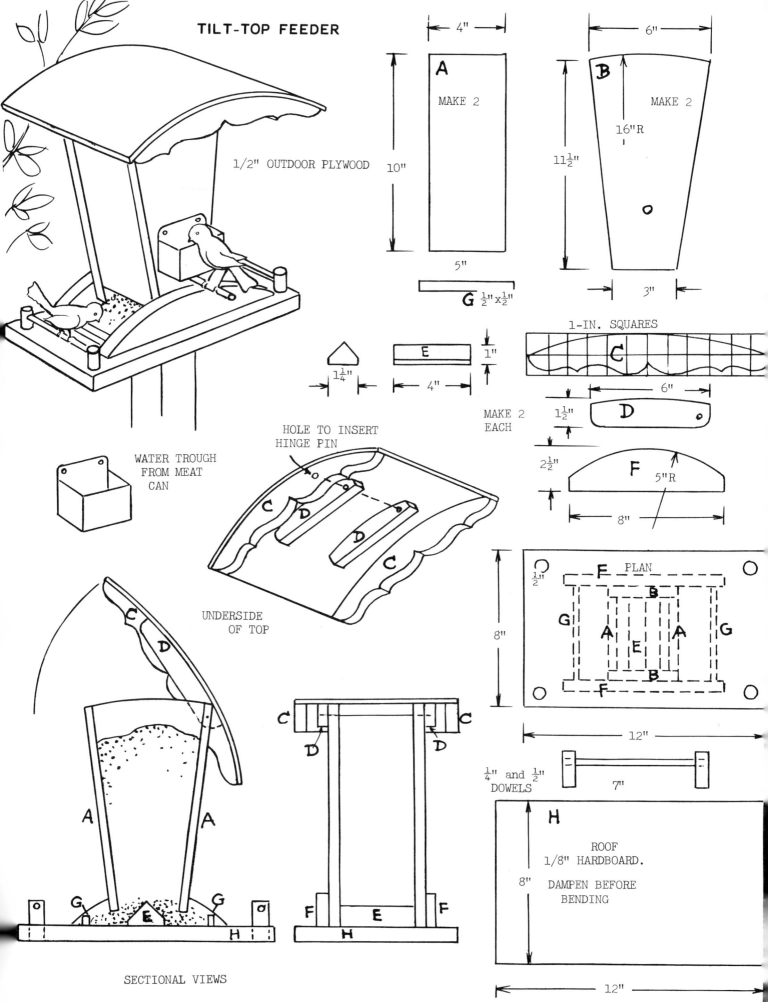

1/2" OUTDOOR PLYWOOD

A — MAKE 2 — 10" — 4" — 5"

G ½" x ½"

B — MAKE 2 — 6" — 11½" — 16"R — 3"

1-IN. SQUARES

C

D

E — 4" — 1"

1¼"

F — 5"R — 2½" — 8"

MAKE 2 EACH — 1½"

WATER TROUGH FROM MEAT CAN

HOLE TO INSERT HINGE PIN

C   D   D   C

UNDERSIDE OF TOP

PLAN

F   B   G   A   E   A   G   G   B   F

½"   8"   12"

¼" and ½" DOWELS — 7"

H
ROOF
1/8" HARDBOARD.

DAMPEN BEFORE BENDING

8"   12"

C   D

A   A

G   E   G   H

C   D   D   C

F   E   F

H

SECTIONAL VIEWS

23

SIMPLE BIRDHOUSE

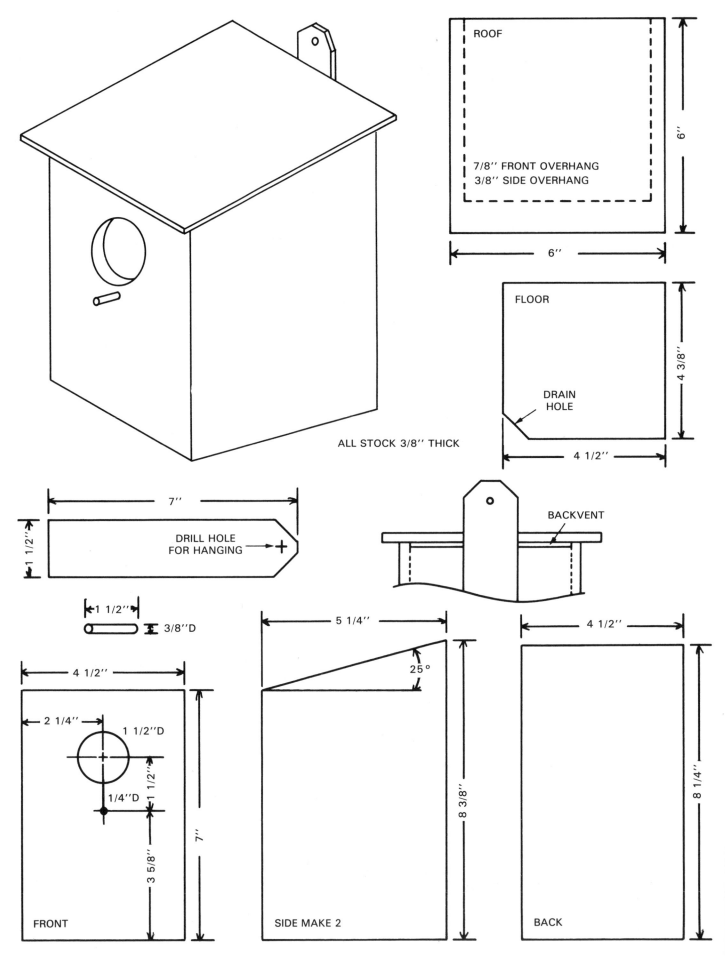

ROOF

7/8'' FRONT OVERHANG
3/8'' SIDE OVERHANG

6''

6''

FLOOR

4 3/8''

DRAIN HOLE

4 1/2''

ALL STOCK 3/8'' THICK

7''

1 1/2''

DRILL HOLE FOR HANGING →

1 1/2''

3/8''D

BACKVENT

5 1/4''

25°

8 3/8''

4 1/2''

8 1/4''

4 1/2''

2 1/4''

1 1/2''D

1/4''D

1 1/2''

3 5/8''

7''

FRONT

SIDE MAKE 2

BACK

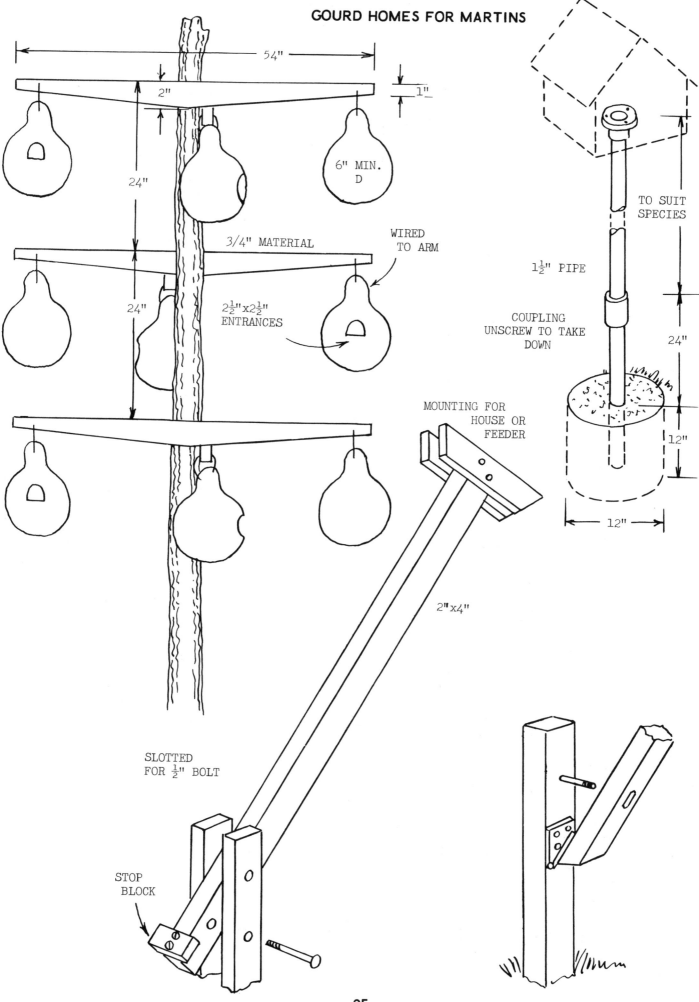

54"

2"

1"

24"

3/4" MATERIAL

WIRED TO ARM

2½"x2½" ENTRANCES

24"

6" MIN. D

TO SUIT SPECIES

1½" PIPE

COUPLING UNSCREW TO TAKE DOWN

24"

12"

12"

MOUNTING FOR HOUSE OR FEEDER

2"x4"

SLOTTED FOR ½" BOLT

STOP BLOCK

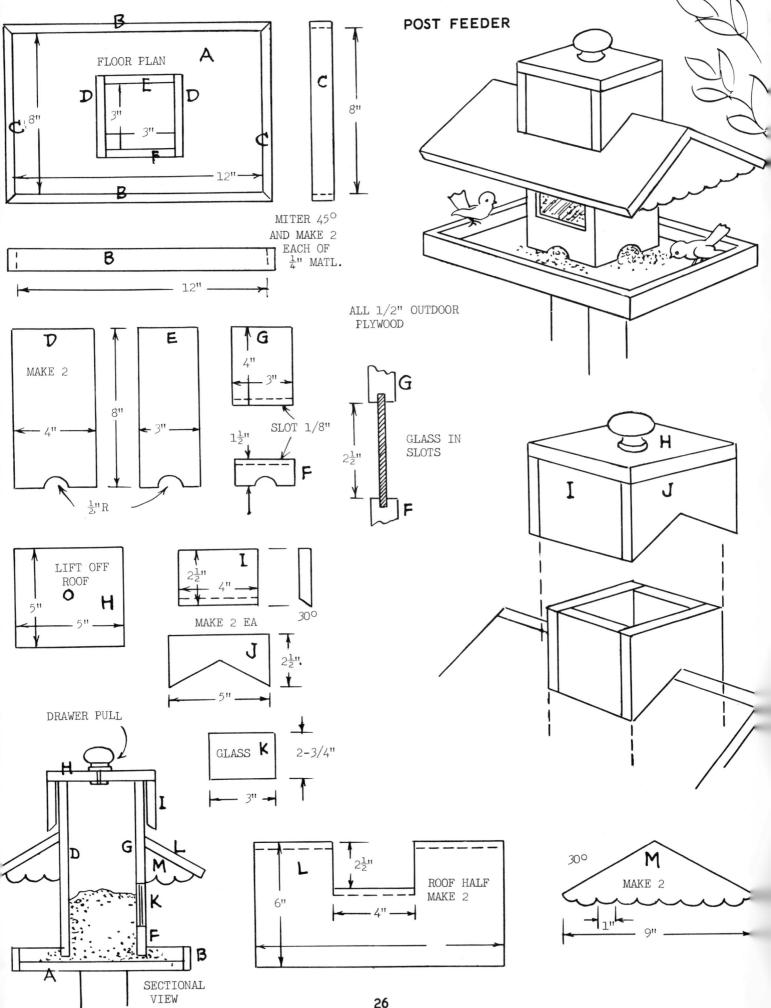

POST FEEDER

FLOOR PLAN A

B

D E D

3" 3"

F

8"

12"

C

B

MITER 45°
AND MAKE 2
EACH OF
¼" MATL.

ALL ½" OUTDOOR
PLYWOOD

C

8"

D

MAKE 2

4"

8"

E

3"

8"

½" R

G

4"

3"

SLOT 1/8"

1½"

F

G

2½"

GLASS IN
SLOTS

F

H

I J

LIFT OFF
ROOF

5"

O H

5"

I

2½"

4"

30°

MAKE 2 EA

J

2½"

5"

DRAWER PULL

H

I

D G L

M

K

F

A B

SECTIONAL
VIEW

GLASS K

2-3/4"

3"

L

2½"

6"

4"

ROOF HALF
MAKE 2

30° M

MAKE 2

1"

9"

26

FOR BLUEBIRD, TREE SWALLOW HOUSE FINCH, CRESTED FLY CATCHER

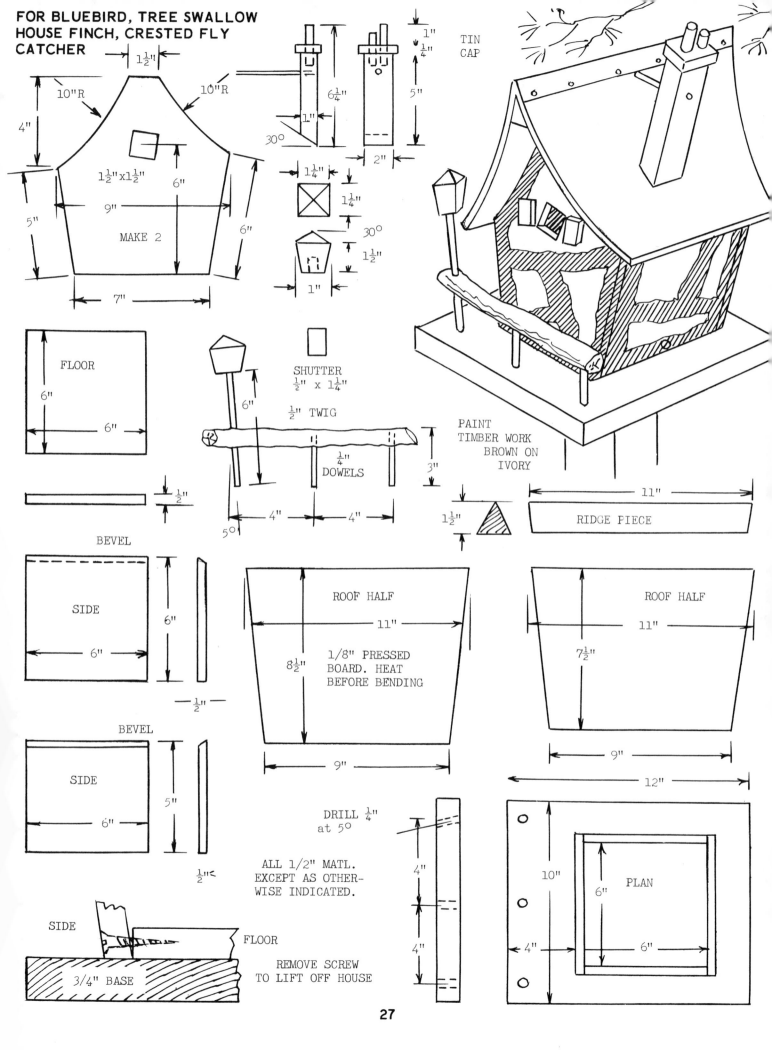

1½"

10"R   10"R

4"

1½"x1½"   6"

5"

9"   6"

MAKE 2

7"

TIN CAP

1"
¼"

6¼"

30°   1"   5"

2"

1¼"

1¼"

30°
1½"

1"

PAINT TIMBER WORK BROWN ON IVORY

FLOOR

6"

6"

½"

BEVEL

SIDE

6"

6"

½"

BEVEL

SIDE

6"

5"

½"

SHUTTER
½" x 1¼"

½" TWIG

6"

¼"
DOWELS

5°   4"   4"

3"

1½"   RIDGE PIECE   11"

ROOF HALF   11"

8½"   1/8" PRESSED BOARD. HEAT BEFORE BENDING

9"

ROOF HALF   11"

7½"

9"

12"

DRILL ¼"
at 5°

ALL 1/2" MATL. EXCEPT AS OTHER-WISE INDICATED.

4"

4"

10"

6"

PLAN

4"   6"

SIDE   FLOOR

3/4" BASE

REMOVE SCREW TO LIFT OFF HOUSE

27

MARTIN COMMUNITY HOUSE

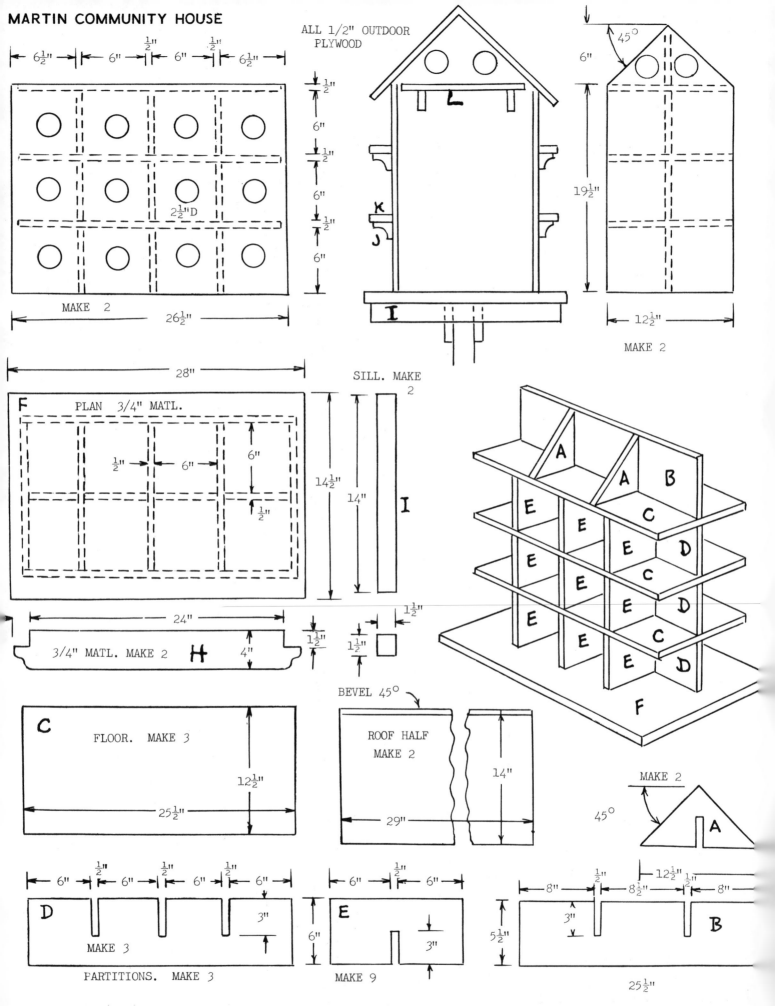

ALL 1/2" OUTDOOR PLYWOOD

$6\frac{1}{2}$" — 6" — $\frac{1}{2}$" — 6" — $\frac{1}{2}$" — $6\frac{1}{2}$"

$\frac{1}{2}$" 6" $\frac{1}{2}$" 6" $\frac{1}{2}$" 6"

$2\frac{1}{2}$"D

MAKE 2 $26\frac{1}{2}$"

L

K
J

I

45°
6"
$19\frac{1}{2}$"
$12\frac{1}{2}$"
MAKE 2

28"

F   PLAN   3/4" MATL.

$\frac{1}{2}$" — 6"   6"
$14\frac{1}{2}$"   14" $\frac{1}{2}$"

SILL. MAKE 2
I

$1\frac{1}{2}$"
$1\frac{1}{2}$" $1\frac{1}{2}$"

24"
3/4" MATL. MAKE 2   H   4"

A   A   B
E   C
E   E   D
E   C
E   E   D
E   C
E   E   D
F

C   FLOOR. MAKE 3
$12\frac{1}{2}$"
$25\frac{1}{2}$"

BEVEL 45°
ROOF HALF MAKE 2
14"
29"

MAKE 2
45°
A

D
6" — $\frac{1}{2}$" — 6" — $\frac{1}{2}$" — 6" — $\frac{1}{2}$" — 6"
3"
MAKE 3
PARTITIONS. MAKE 3

E
6" — $\frac{1}{2}$" — 6"
6"
3"
MAKE 9

B
8" — $\frac{1}{2}$" — $12\frac{1}{2}$" — $\frac{1}{2}$" — 8"
$8\frac{1}{2}$"
3"
$5\frac{1}{2}$"
$25\frac{1}{2}$"

Martin Community house.

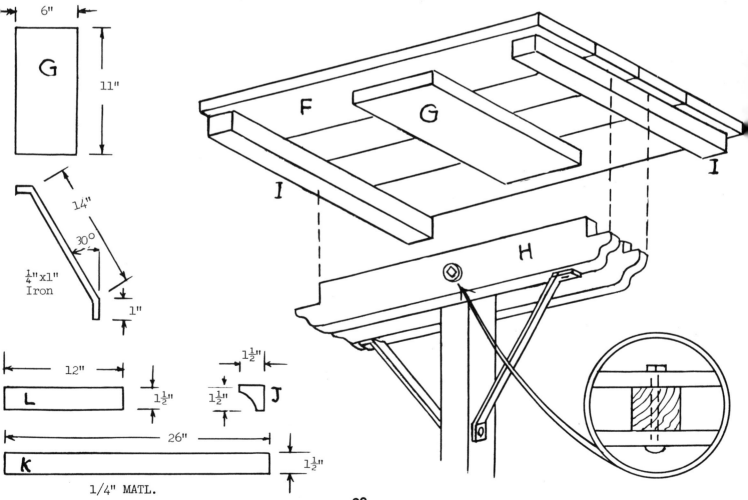

29

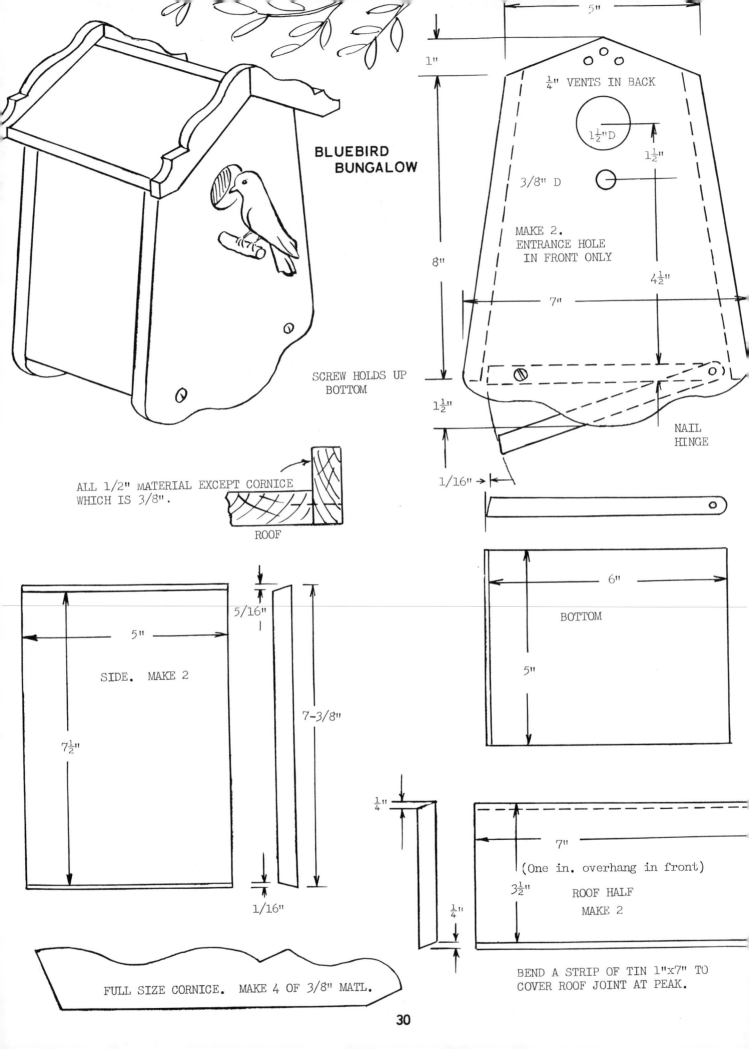

BLUEBIRD
BUNGALOW

SCREW HOLDS UP
BOTTOM

ALL 1/2" MATERIAL EXCEPT CORNICE
WHICH IS 3/8".

ROOF

5"

1"

8"

1/4" VENTS IN BACK

1 1/2"D

3/8" D

1 1/2"

MAKE 2.
ENTRANCE HOLE
IN FRONT ONLY

4 1/2"

7"

1 1/2"

1/16"

NAIL
HINGE

SIDE. MAKE 2

5"

7 1/2"

5/16"

7-3/8"

1/16"

6"

BOTTOM

5"

1/4"

1/4"

7"

(One in. overhang in front)

3 1/2"

ROOF HALF

MAKE 2

FULL SIZE CORNICE. MAKE 4 OF 3/8" MATL.

BEND A STRIP OF TIN 1"x7" TO
COVER ROOF JOINT AT PEAK.

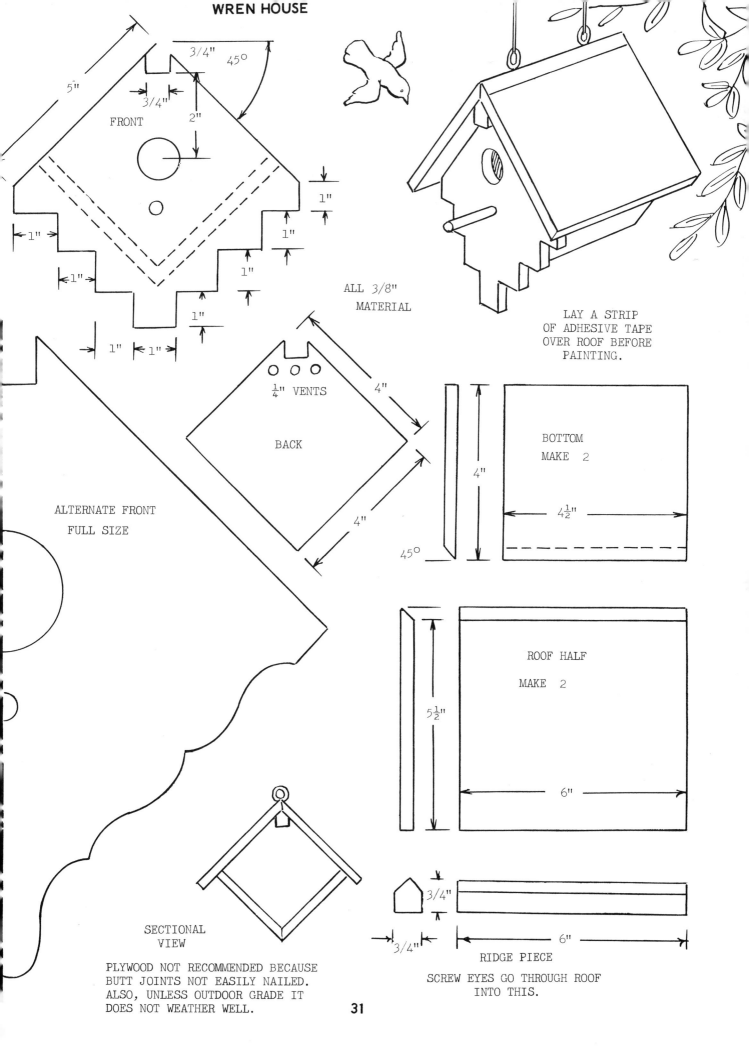

WREN HOUSE

FRONT

5"

3/4"   45°

3/4"

2"

1"

1"

1"

1"

1"

1"

1"

ALL 3/8"
MATERIAL

LAY A STRIP
OF ADHESIVE TAPE
OVER ROOF BEFORE
PAINTING.

¼" VENTS

4"

BACK

4"

4"

45°

4"

BOTTOM
MAKE 2

4½"

ALTERNATE FRONT
FULL SIZE

5½"

ROOF HALF

MAKE 2

6"

SECTIONAL
VIEW

3/4"

3/4"

6"

RIDGE PIECE

PLYWOOD NOT RECOMMENDED BECAUSE
BUTT JOINTS NOT EASILY NAILED.
ALSO, UNLESS OUTDOOR GRADE IT
DOES NOT WEATHER WELL.

SCREW EYES GO THROUGH ROOF
INTO THIS.

31

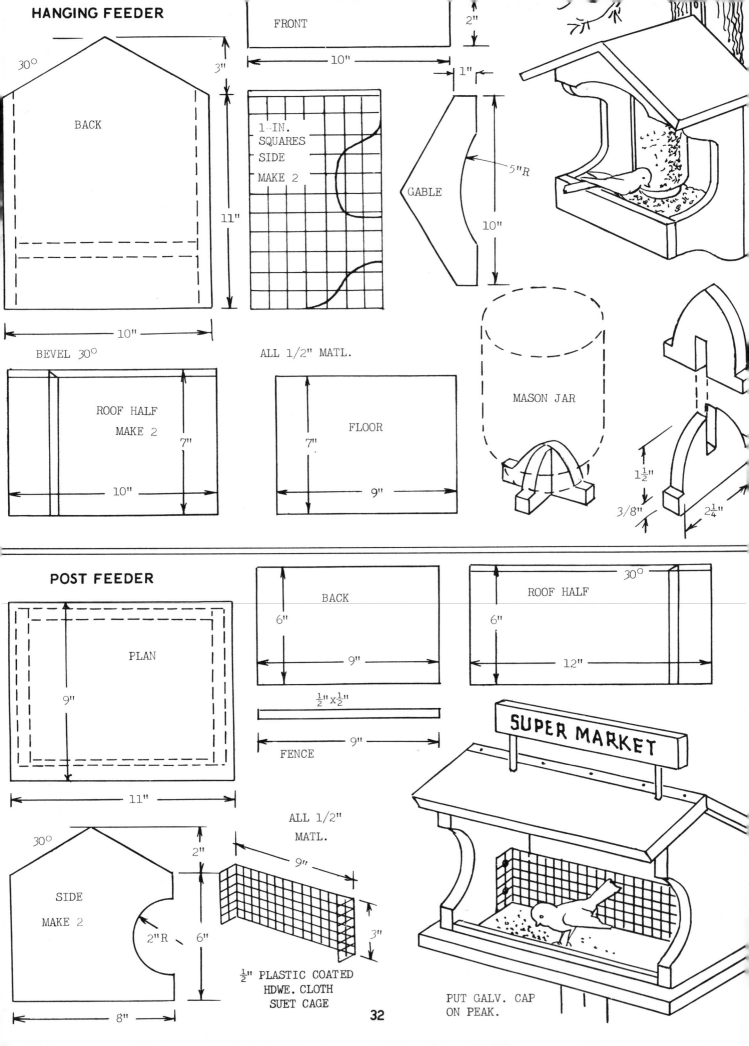

HANGING FEEDER

FRONT

2"

BACK

30°

3"

10"

11"

1"

1-IN. SQUARES
SIDE
MAKE 2

5"R

GABLE

10"

10"

BEVEL 30°

ALL 1/2" MATL.

MASON JAR

ROOF HALF
MAKE 2

7"

FLOOR

7"

10"

9"

1½"

3/8"

2¼"

POST FEEDER

PLAN

9"

11"

BACK

6"

9"

½" x ½"

FENCE

9"

ROOF HALF

30°

6"

12"

SUPER MARKET

30°

SIDE
MAKE 2

2"R

2"

6"

8"

ALL 1/2"
MATL.

9"

3"

½" PLASTIC COATED
HDWE. CLOTH
SUET CAGE

PUT GALV. CAP
ON PEAK.

32

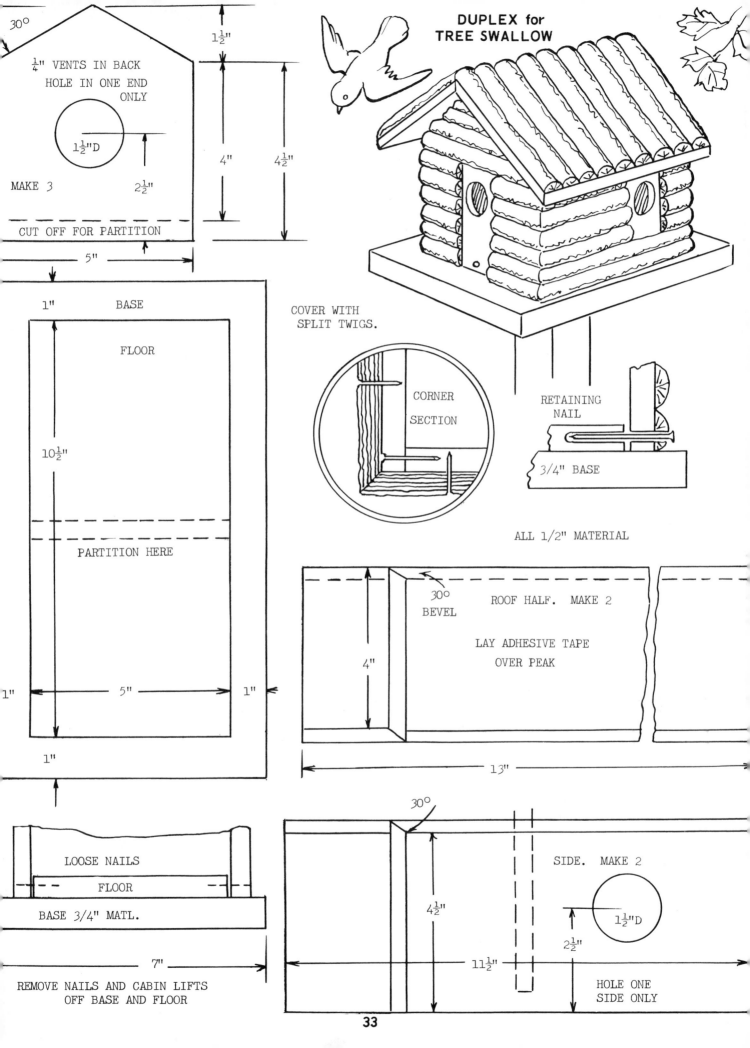

30°

¼" VENTS IN BACK
HOLE IN ONE END
ONLY

1½"D

MAKE 3

2½"

CUT OFF FOR PARTITION

1½"

4"

4½"

5"

DUPLEX for
TREE SWALLOW

COVER WITH
SPLIT TWIGS.

CORNER
SECTION

RETAINING
NAIL

3/4" BASE

ALL 1/2" MATERIAL

1"   BASE

FLOOR

10½"

PARTITION HERE

1"   5"   1"

1"

30°
BEVEL

ROOF HALF. MAKE 2

LAY ADHESIVE TAPE
OVER PEAK

4"

13"

LOOSE NAILS

FLOOR

BASE 3/4" MATL.

7"

REMOVE NAILS AND CABIN LIFTS
OFF BASE AND FLOOR

30°

4½"

11½"

SIDE. MAKE 2

1½"D

2½"

HOLE ONE
SIDE ONLY

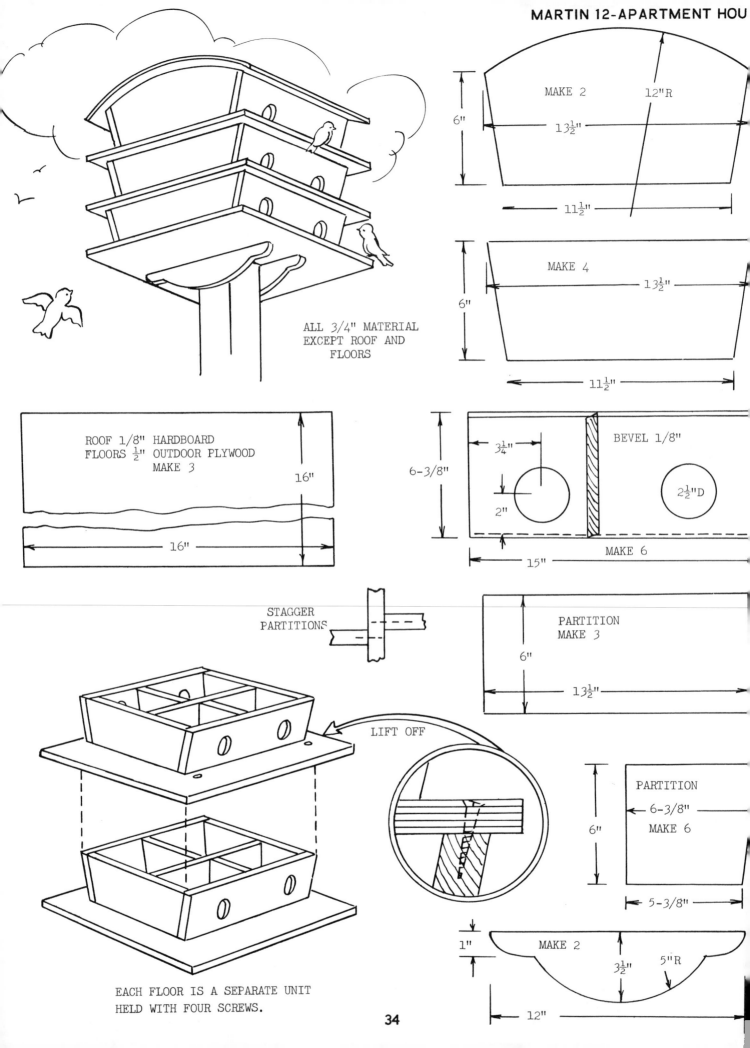

MAKE 2
12"R
6"
13½"
11½"

MAKE 4
13½"
6"
11½"

ALL 3/4" MATERIAL
EXCEPT ROOF AND
FLOORS

ROOF 1/8" HARDBOARD
FLOORS ½" OUTDOOR PLYWOOD
MAKE 3
16"
16"

BEVEL 1/8"
6-3/8"
3¼"
2"
2½"D
15"
MAKE 6

STAGGER
PARTITIONS

PARTITION
MAKE 3
6"
13½"

LIFT OFF

PARTITION
6-3/8"
6"
MAKE 6
5-3/8"

MAKE 2
1"
3½"
5"R
12"

EACH FLOOR IS A SEPARATE UNIT
HELD WITH FOUR SCREWS.

34

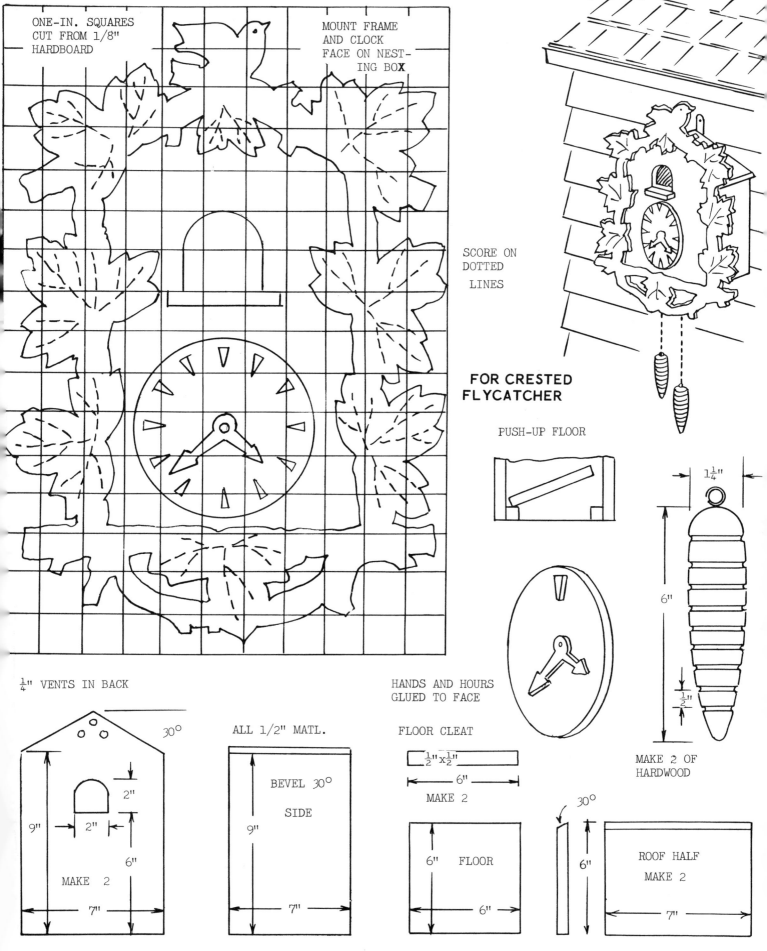

ONE-IN. SQUARES
CUT FROM 1/8"
HARDBOARD

MOUNT FRAME
AND CLOCK
FACE ON NEST-
ING BOX

SCORE ON
DOTTED
LINES

**FOR CRESTED
FLYCATCHER**

PUSH-UP FLOOR

1¼"

6"

½"

¼" VENTS IN BACK

HANDS AND HOURS
GLUED TO FACE

MAKE 2 OF
HARDWOOD

30°

2"

2"

9"

6"

MAKE 2

7"

ALL 1/2" MATL.

BEVEL 30°

SIDE

9"

7"

FLOOR CLEAT

½"x½"

6"

MAKE 2

6" FLOOR

6"

30°

6"

ROOF HALF

MAKE 2

7"

MAKE THE COMPLETE NESTING BOX AND SECURE LEAFY FRAME AND CLOCK FACE TO FRONT.
DUMMY WEIGHTS ARE LATHE-TURNED HARDWOOD, HUNG WITH LIGHT CHAINS. CLOCK HANDS
AND HOUR MARKERS SHOULD BE ENAMELED IVORY. MAHOGANY OR WALNUT STAIN ON WOOD.

PAINT ROOF GREEN
AFTER LAYING ADHESIDE
TAPE OVER PEAK

DUPLEX WITH BREEZEWAY
FOR CAROLINA WREN

AN AIRY APARTMENT FOR
CONGENIAL TENANTS. HALF-
INCH MATERIAL IS USED THRU-
OUT EXCEPT FOR THE CUPOLA,
WHICH IS A SOLID BLOCK. THE
HOUSE CAN BE LIFTED OFF BY
REMOVING LOOSE NAILS OR
SCREWS IN ENDS, AS SHOWN IN
CIRCLE.

PAINT WALLS IVORY,
DUMMY WINDOWS STENCILLED
IN BLACK OR DARK BLUE.

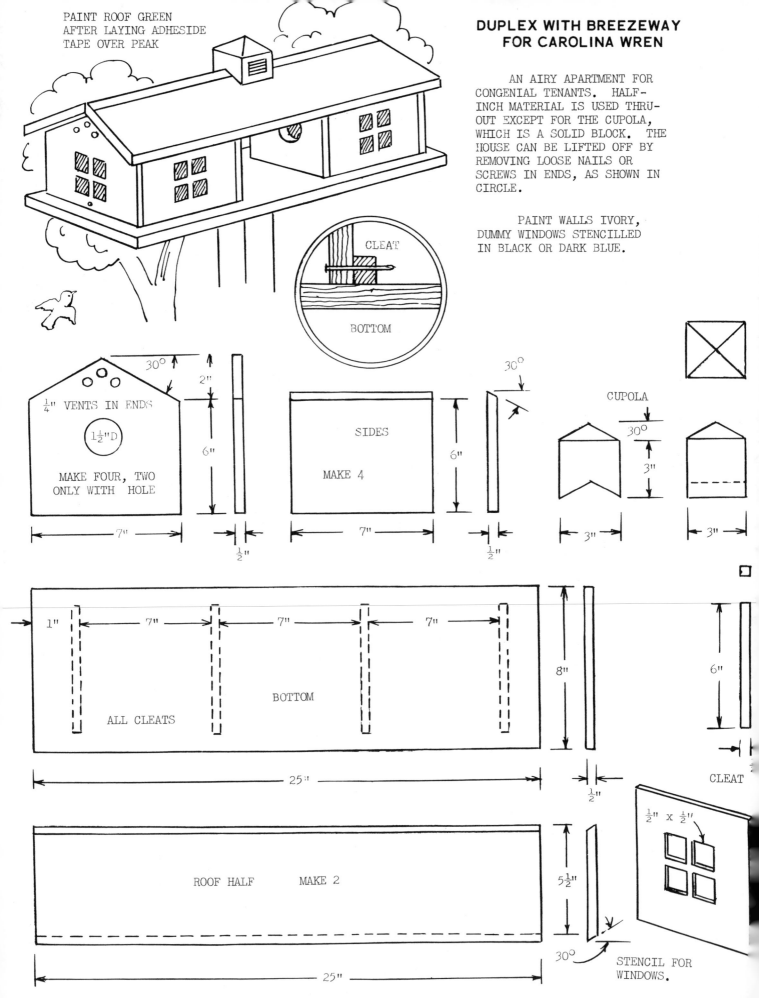

CLEAT

BOTTOM

30°
2"
$\frac{1}{4}$" VENTS IN ENDS
$1\frac{1}{2}$"D
6"
MAKE FOUR, TWO
ONLY WITH HOLE
7"
$\frac{1}{2}$"

SIDES
MAKE 4
30°
6"
7"
$\frac{1}{2}$"

CUPOLA
30°
3"
3"
3"

1"
7"
7"
7"
ALL CLEATS
BOTTOM
25"
8"
$\frac{1}{2}$"
6"
CLEAT

ROOF HALF   MAKE 2
$5\frac{1}{2}$"
30°
25"

$\frac{1}{2}$" X $\frac{1}{2}$"
STENCIL FOR
WINDOWS.

36

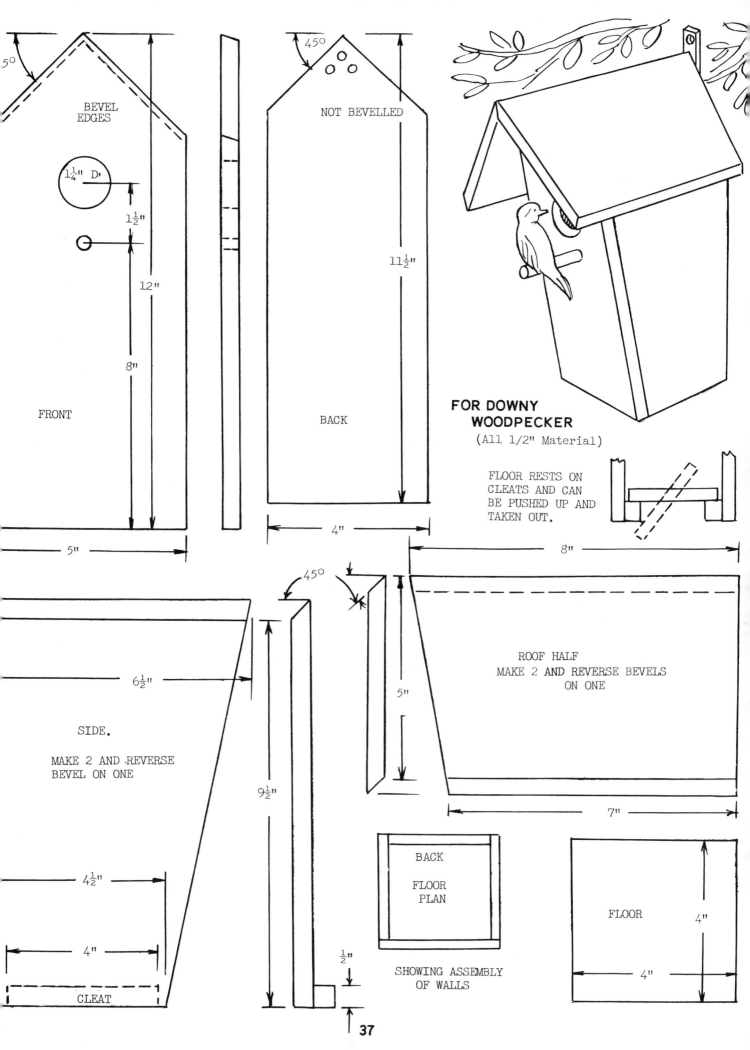

5°

BEVEL
EDGES

1¼" D

1½"

12"

8"

FRONT

5"

NOT BEVELLED

45°

11½"

4"

BACK

**FOR DOWNY
WOODPECKER**

(All 1/2" Material)

FLOOR RESTS ON
CLEATS AND CAN
BE PUSHED UP AND
TAKEN OUT.

8"

45°

6½"

SIDE.

MAKE 2 AND REVERSE
BEVEL ON ONE

9½"

5"

ROOF HALF
MAKE 2 AND REVERSE BEVELS
ON ONE

7"

4½"

4"

½"

CLEAT

BACK

FLOOR
PLAN

SHOWING ASSEMBLY
OF WALLS

FLOOR

4"

4"

SHINGLED BIRDHOUSE

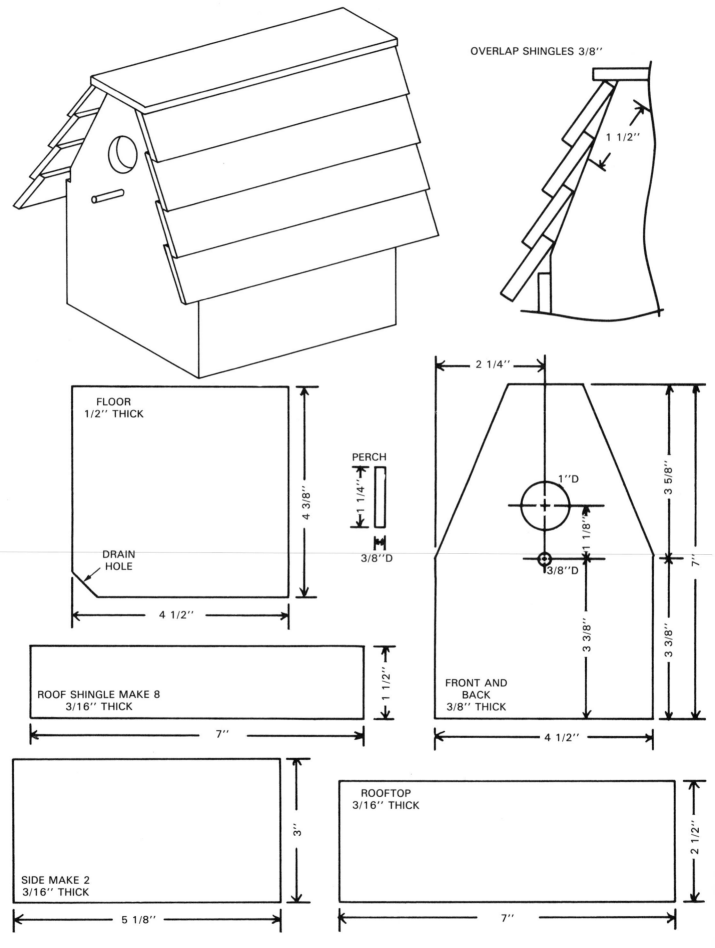

OVERLAP SHINGLES 3/8''

1 1/2''

FLOOR
1/2'' THICK

4 3/8''

DRAIN
HOLE

4 1/2''

PERCH

1 1/4''

3/8''D

ROOF SHINGLE MAKE 8
3/16'' THICK

1 1/2''

7''

2 1/4''

1''D

1 1/8''

3/8''D

3 5/8''

7''

3 3/8''

3 3/8''

FRONT AND
BACK
3/8'' THICK

4 1/2''

SIDE MAKE 2
3/16'' THICK

3''

5 1/8''

ROOFTOP
3/16'' THICK

2 1/2''

7''

38

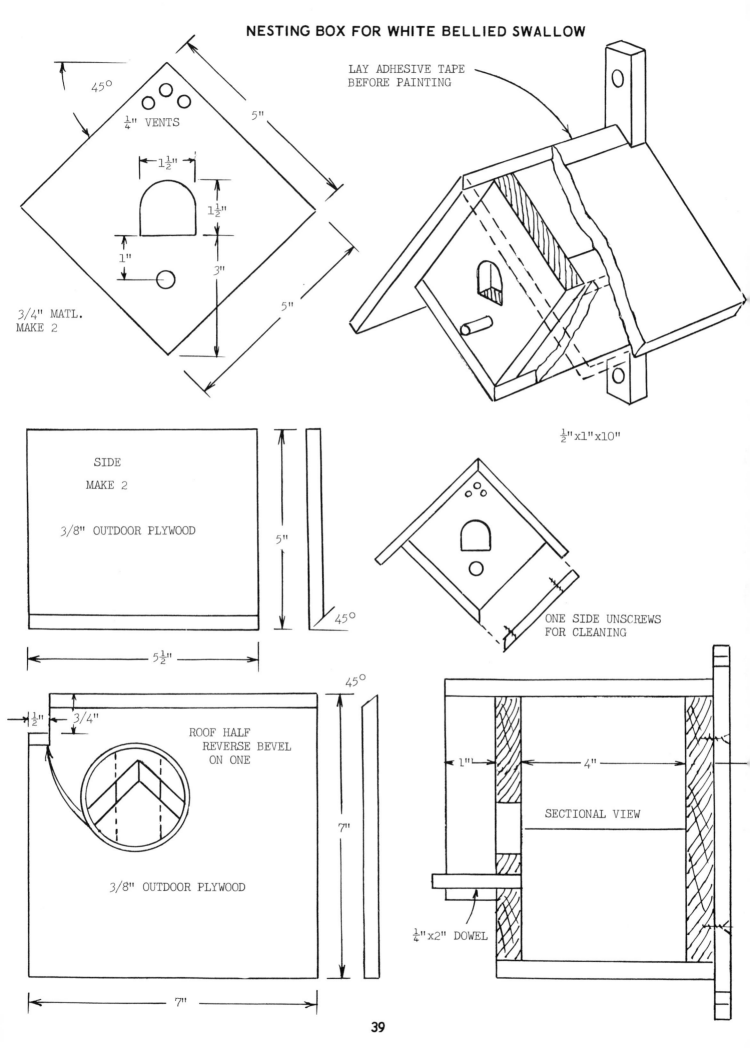

NESTING BOX FOR WHITE BELLIED SWALLOW

45°

¼" VENTS

5"

1½"

1½"

1"

3"

5"

3/4" MATL.
MAKE 2

LAY ADHESIVE TAPE
BEFORE PAINTING

½"x1"x10"

SIDE
MAKE 2

3/8" OUTDOOR PLYWOOD

5"

45°

5½"

ONE SIDE UNSCREWS
FOR CLEANING

45°

½"

3/4"

ROOF HALF
REVERSE BEVEL
ON ONE

7"

3/8" OUTDOOR PLYWOOD

7"

1"

4"

SECTIONAL VIEW

¼"x2" DOWEL

39

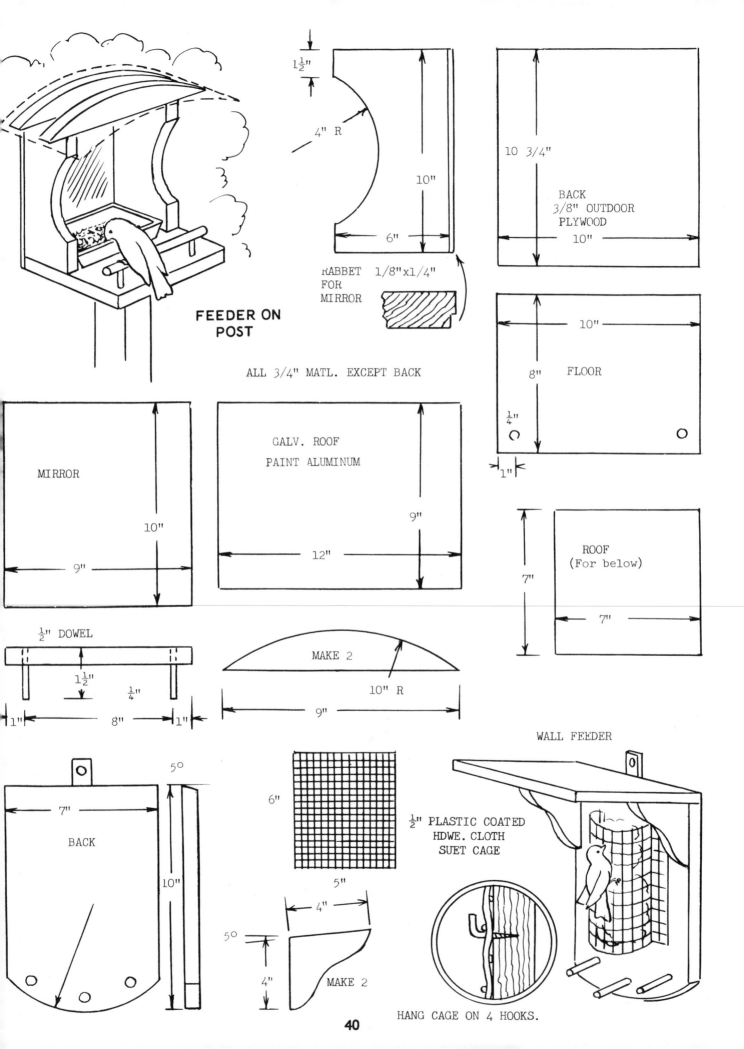

FEEDER ON POST

1½"

4" R

10"

6"

RABBET 1/8"x1/4"
FOR
MIRROR

ALL 3/4" MATL. EXCEPT BACK

10 3/4"

BACK
3/8" OUTDOOR
PLYWOOD

10"

10"

8" FLOOR

¼"

1"

MIRROR

10"

9"

GALV. ROOF
PAINT ALUMINUM

9"

12"

ROOF
(For below)

7"

7"

½" DOWEL

1½"

¼"

1" 8" 1"

MAKE 2

10" R

9"

WALL FEEDER

BACK

7"

10"

5°

6"

5"

4"

5°

4"

MAKE 2

½" PLASTIC COATED
HDWE. CLOTH
SUET CAGE

HANG CAGE ON 4 HOOKS.

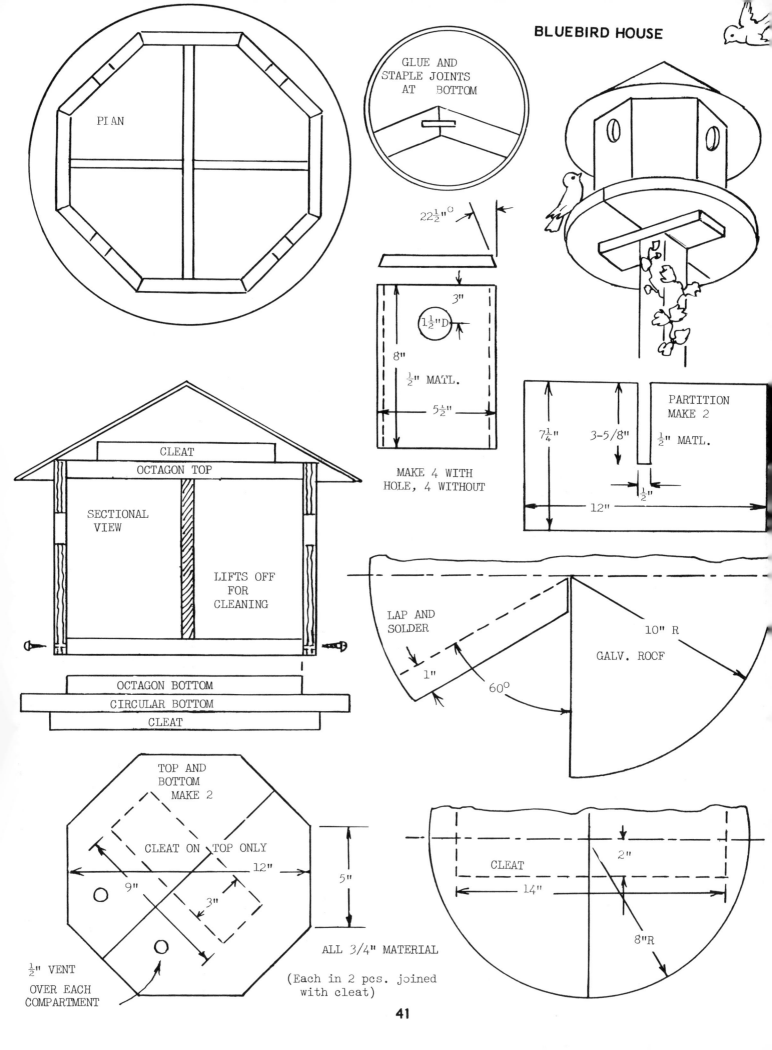

BLUEBIRD HOUSE

PLAN

GLUE AND
STAPLE JOINTS
AT BOTTOM

$22\frac{1}{2}$"°

$1\frac{1}{2}$"D   3"

8"

$\frac{1}{2}$" MATL.

$5\frac{1}{2}$"

MAKE 4 WITH
HOLE, 4 WITHOUT

PARTITION
MAKE 2

$\frac{1}{2}$" MATL.

$7\frac{1}{4}$"   3-5/8"

$\frac{1}{2}$"

12"

CLEAT
OCTAGON TOP

SECTIONAL
VIEW

LIFTS OFF
FOR
CLEANING

OCTAGON BOTTOM
CIRCULAR BOTTOM
CLEAT

LAP AND
SOLDER

1"

60°

10" R

GALV. ROOF

TOP AND
BOTTOM
MAKE 2

CLEAT ON TOP ONLY

12"

9"

3"

5"

ALL 3/4" MATERIAL

(Each in 2 pcs. joined
with cleat)

$\frac{1}{2}$" VENT

OVER EACH
COMPARTMENT

CLEAT

2"

14"

8"R

41

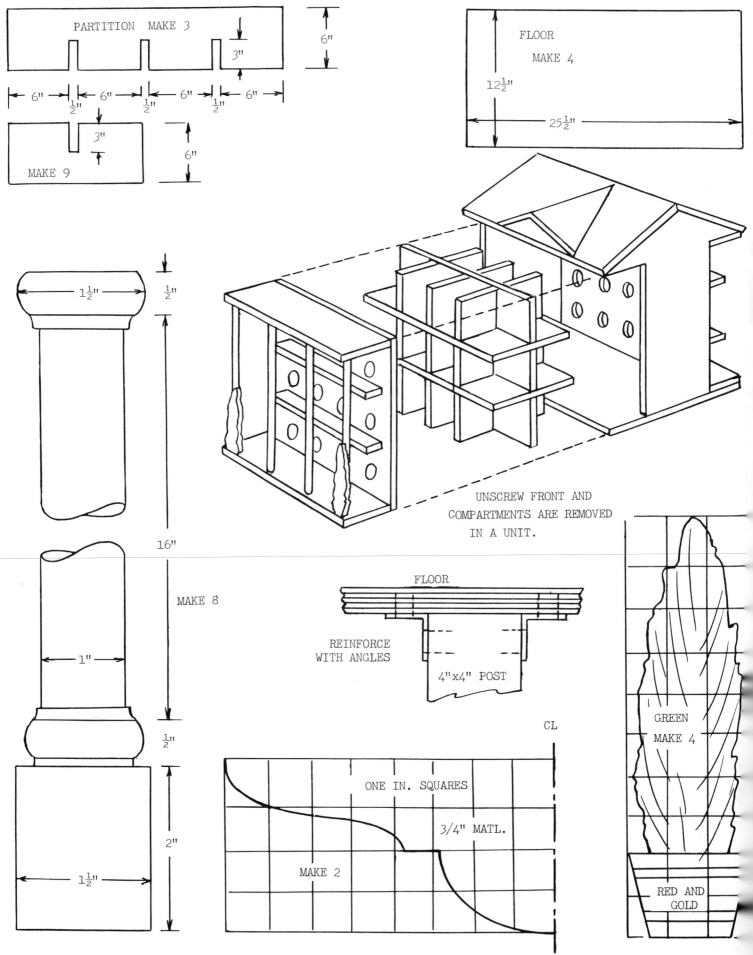

PARTITION MAKE 3

6"

3"

6"   6"   6"   6"

½"   ½"   ½"

3"

6"

MAKE 9

FLOOR

MAKE 4

12½"

25½"

1½"

½"

16"

MAKE 8

1"

½"

2"

1½"

UNSCREW FRONT AND
COMPARTMENTS ARE REMOVED
IN A UNIT.

FLOOR

REINFORCE
WITH ANGLES

4"x4" POST

CL

ONE IN. SQUARES

3/4" MATL.

MAKE 2

GREEN

MAKE 4

RED AND
GOLD

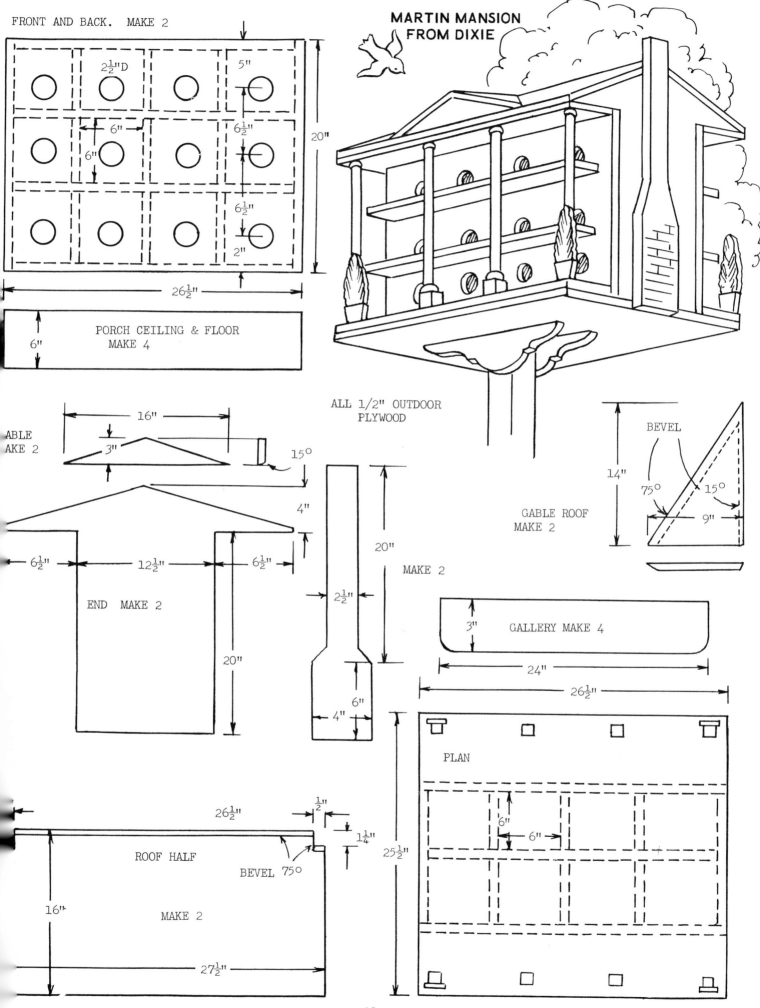

FRONT AND BACK. MAKE 2

MARTIN MANSION
FROM DIXIE

2½"D

5"

6"

6½"

6"

6½"

2"

20"

26½"

PORCH CEILING & FLOOR
MAKE 4

6"

ALL 1/2" OUTDOOR
PLYWOOD

ABLE
AKE 2

16"

3"

15°

4"

6½"

12½"

6½"

END MAKE 2

20"

20"

MAKE 2

2½"

6"

4"

BEVEL

14"

75°

15°

9"

GABLE ROOF
MAKE 2

3"

GALLERY MAKE 4

24"

26½"

PLAN

6"

6"

25½"

½"

1¼"

26½"

ROOF HALF

BEVEL 75°

16"

MAKE 2

27½"

43

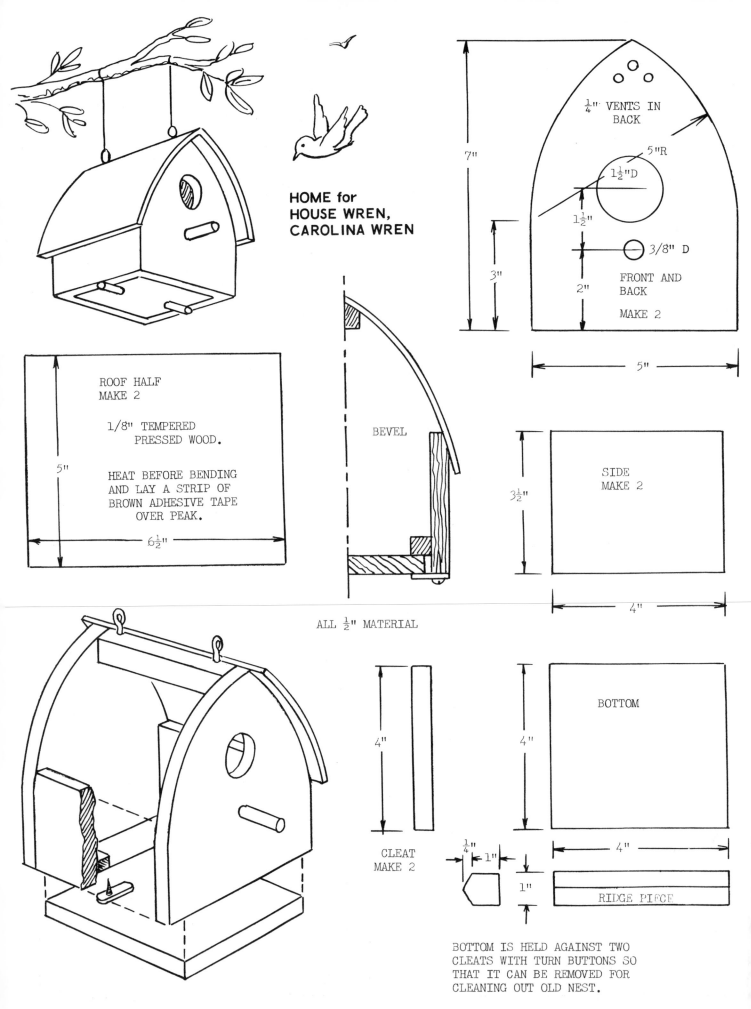

HOME for HOUSE WREN, CAROLINA WREN

¼" VENTS IN BACK

7"

5"R

1½"D

1½"

3"

3/8" D

2"

FRONT AND BACK

MAKE 2

5"

ROOF HALF
MAKE 2

1/8" TEMPERED
PRESSED WOOD.

HEAT BEFORE BENDING
AND LAY A STRIP OF
BROWN ADHESIVE TAPE
OVER PEAK.

5"

6½"

BEVEL

SIDE
MAKE 2

3½"

4"

ALL ½" MATERIAL

4"

CLEAT
MAKE 2

BOTTOM

4"

4"

¼"

1"

1"

RIDGE PIECE

BOTTOM IS HELD AGAINST TWO
CLEATS WITH TURN BUTTONS SO
THAT IT CAN BE REMOVED FOR
CLEANING OUT OLD NEST.

For HOUSE FINCH

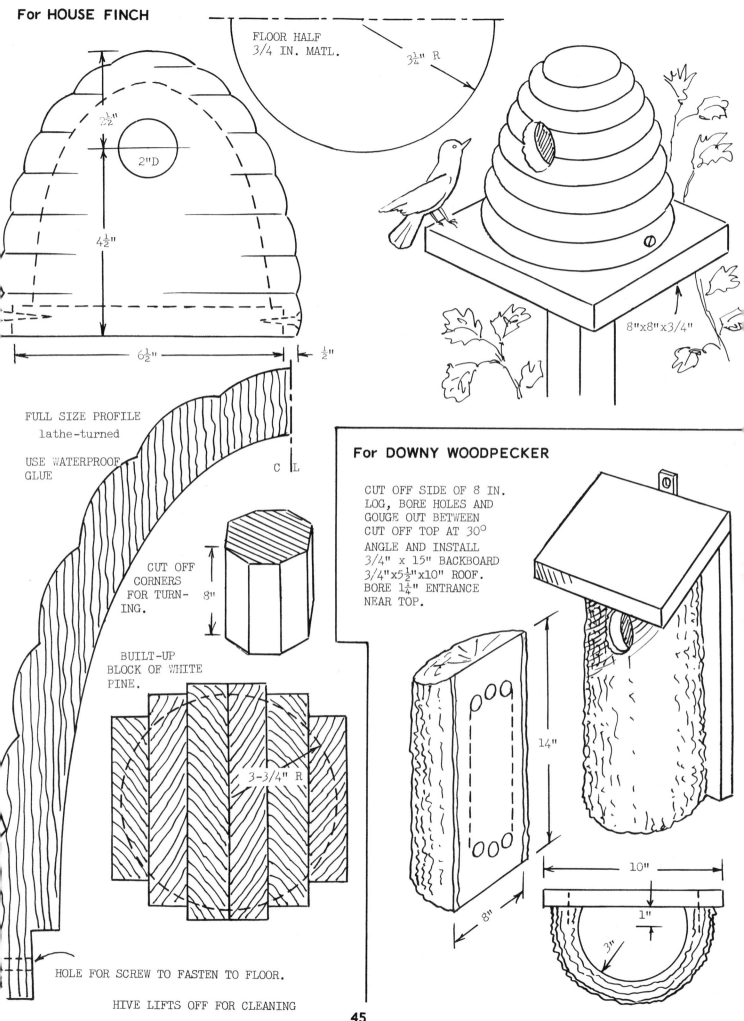

FLOOR HALF
3/4 IN. MATL.

$3\frac{1}{4}$" R

$2\frac{1}{2}$"

2"D

$4\frac{1}{2}$"

$6\frac{1}{2}$"

$\frac{1}{2}$"

FULL SIZE PROFILE
lathe-turned

USE WATERPROOF
GLUE

C L

CUT OFF
CORNERS
FOR TURN-
ING.

8"

BUILT-UP
BLOCK OF WHITE
PINE.

3-3/4" R

HOLE FOR SCREW TO FASTEN TO FLOOR.

HIVE LIFTS OFF FOR CLEANING

8"x8"x3/4"

For DOWNY WOODPECKER

CUT OFF SIDE OF 8 IN.
LOG, BORE HOLES AND
GOUGE OUT BETWEEN
CUT OFF TOP AT 30°
ANGLE AND INSTALL
3/4" x 15" BACKBOARD
3/4"x5½"x10" ROOF.
BORE 1¼" ENTRANCE
NEAR TOP.

14"

8"

10"

1"

3"

45

BIRD BARN

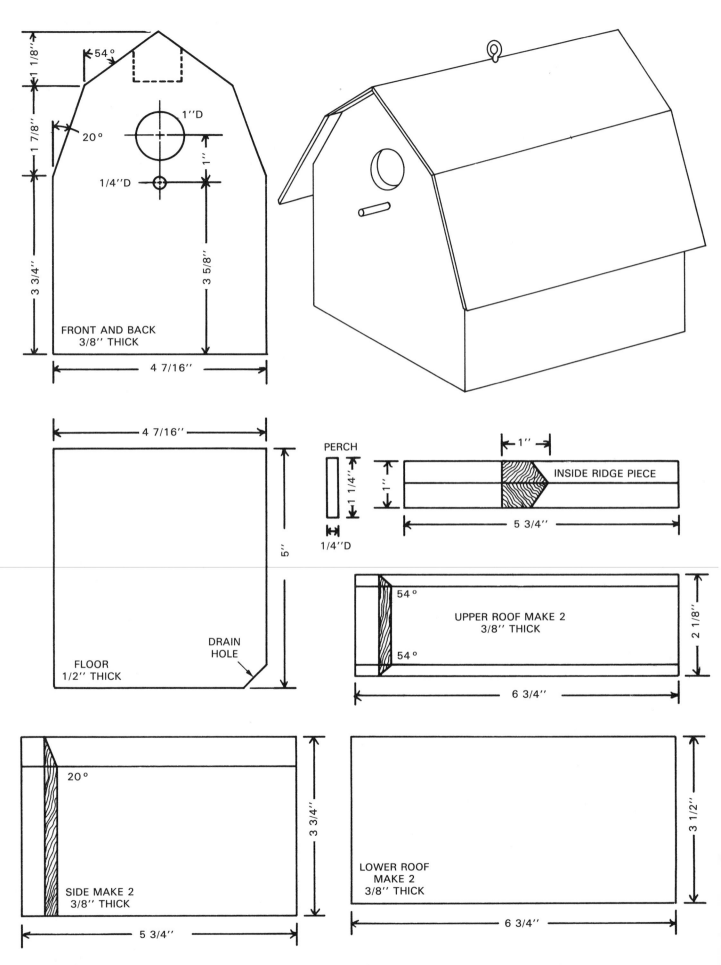

54°

1 1/8''

1 7/8''

20°

1''D

1/4''D

1''

3 3/4''

3 5/8''

FRONT AND BACK
3/8'' THICK

4 7/16''

4 7/16''

5''

PERCH

1 1/4''

1/4''D

1''

1''

INSIDE RIDGE PIECE

5 3/4''

DRAIN
HOLE

FLOOR
1/2'' THICK

54°

54°

UPPER ROOF MAKE 2
3/8'' THICK

2 1/8''

6 3/4''

20°

3 3/4''

SIDE MAKE 2
3/8'' THICK

5 3/4''

LOWER ROOF
MAKE 2
3/8'' THICK

3 1/2''

6 3/4''

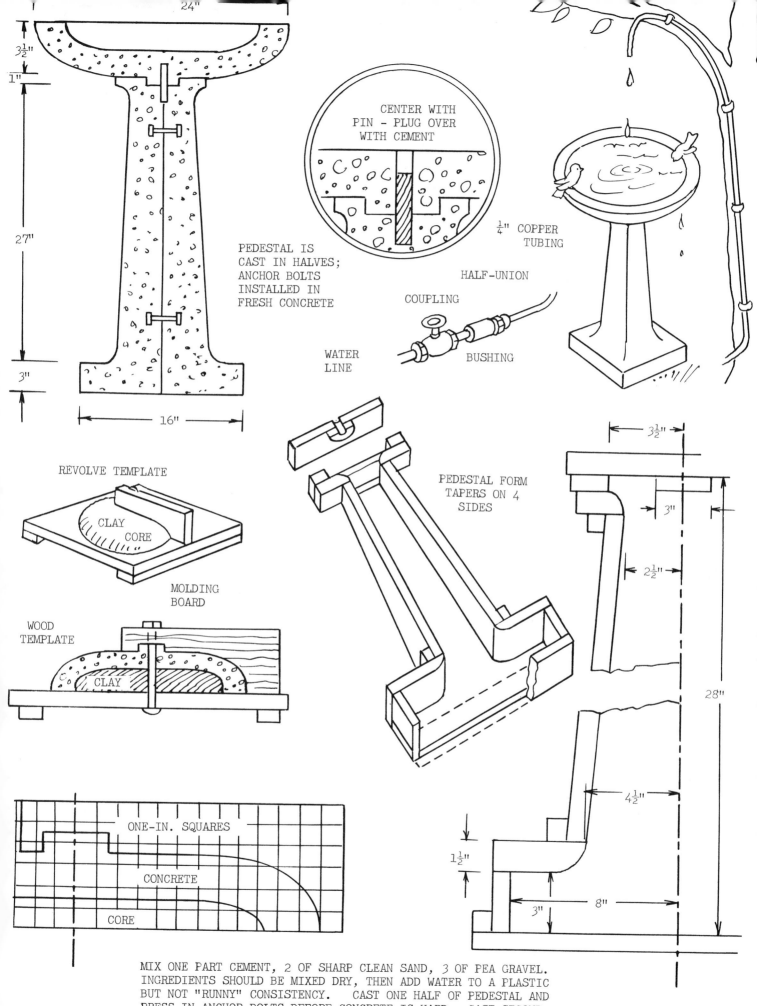

24"

3½"

1"

27"

3"

16"

CENTER WITH
PIN - PLUG OVER
WITH CEMENT

PEDESTAL IS
CAST IN HALVES;
ANCHOR BOLTS
INSTALLED IN
FRESH CONCRETE

¼" COPPER
TUBING

HALF-UNION

COUPLING

WATER
LINE

BUSHING

REVOLVE TEMPLATE

CLAY
CORE

MOLDING
BOARD

WOOD
TEMPLATE

CLAY

PEDESTAL FORM
TAPERS ON 4
SIDES

3½"

3"

2½"

28"

4½"

1½"

3"   8"

ONE-IN. SQUARES

CONCRETE

CORE

MIX ONE PART CEMENT, 2 OF SHARP CLEAN SAND, 3 OF PEA GRAVEL.
INGREDIENTS SHOULD BE MIXED DRY, THEN ADD WATER TO A PLASTIC
BUT NOT "RUNNY" CONSISTENCY.   CAST ONE HALF OF PEDESTAL AND
PRESS IN ANCHOR BOLTS BEFORE CONCRETE IS HARD.   CAST SECOND
HALF AND PLACE FIRST OVER IT.   KEEP CONCRETE MOIST 48 HOURS.

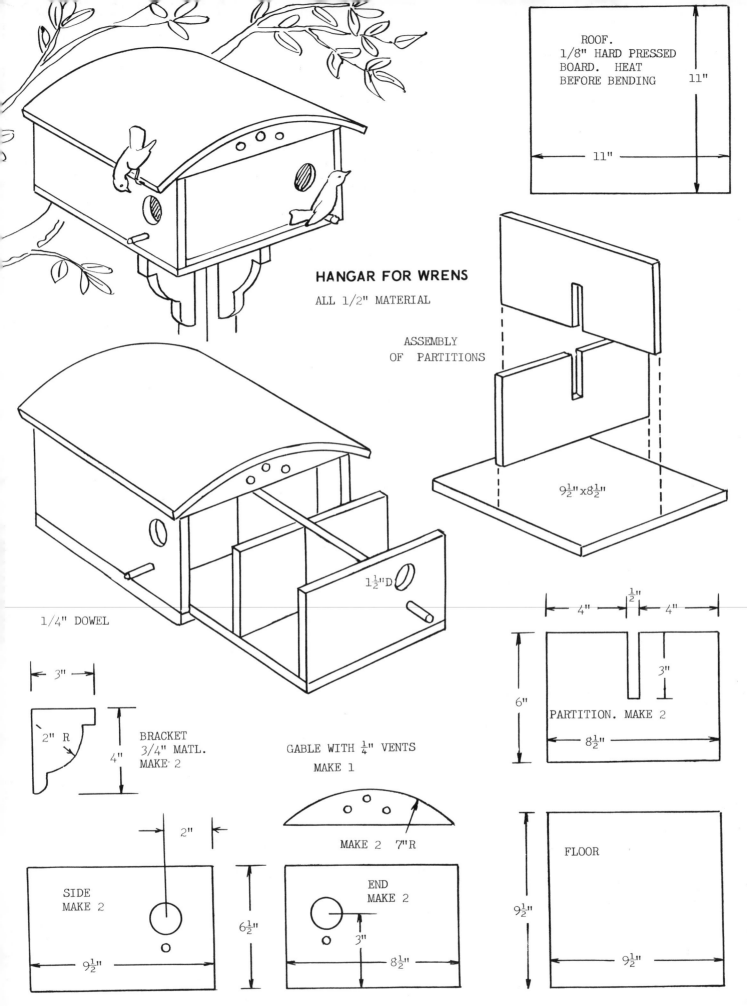

ROOF.
1/8" HARD PRESSED
BOARD. HEAT
BEFORE BENDING

11"

11"

HANGAR FOR WRENS

ALL 1/2" MATERIAL

ASSEMBLY
OF PARTITIONS

$9\frac{1}{2}$"x$8\frac{1}{2}$"

$1\frac{1}{2}$"D

1/4" DOWEL

3"

2" R

BRACKET
3/4" MATL.
MAKE 2

4"

4" $\frac{1}{2}$"   4"

6"

3"

PARTITION. MAKE 2

$8\frac{1}{2}$"

GABLE WITH $\frac{1}{4}$" VENTS

MAKE 1

MAKE 2   7"R

2"

SIDE
MAKE 2

$6\frac{1}{2}$"

$9\frac{1}{2}$"

END
MAKE 2

3"

$8\frac{1}{2}$"

FLOOR

$9\frac{1}{2}$"

$9\frac{1}{2}$"

BLUEBIRD HOUSE

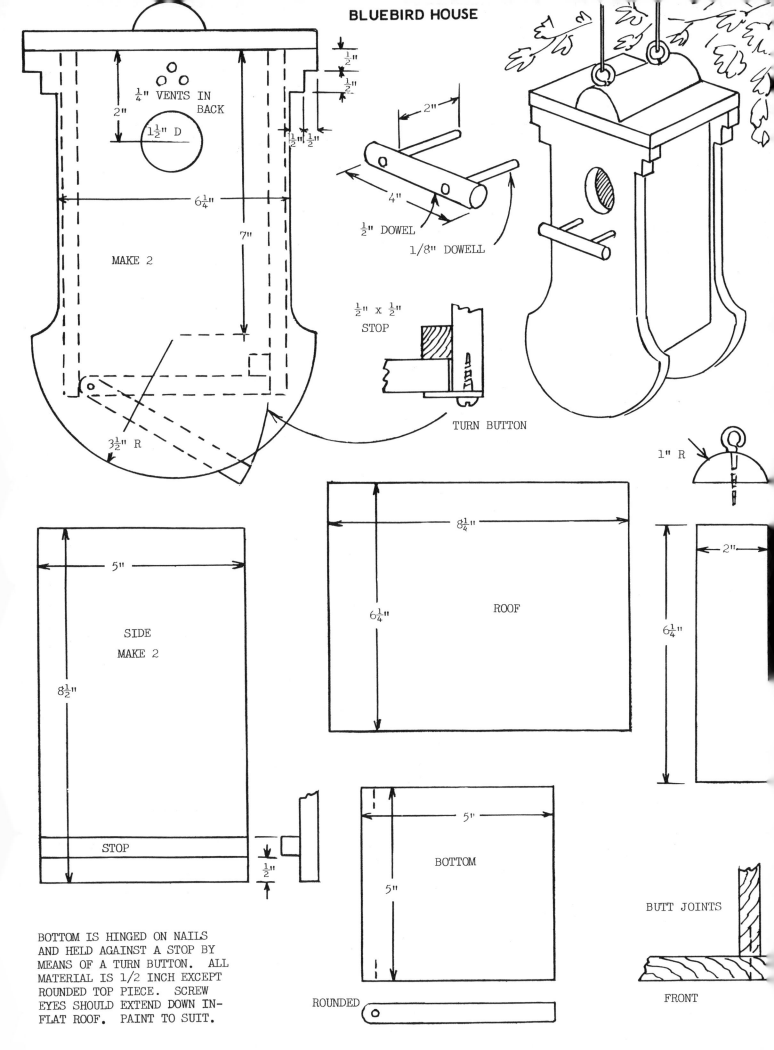

$\frac{1}{4}$" VENTS IN BACK

2"

$1\frac{1}{2}$" D

$\frac{1}{2}$" $\frac{1}{2}$"

$\frac{1}{2}$" $\frac{1}{2}$"

6$\frac{1}{4}$"

7"

MAKE 2

3$\frac{1}{2}$" R

2"

$\frac{1}{2}$" DOWEL

1/8" DOWELL

$\frac{1}{2}$" x $\frac{1}{2}$" STOP

TURN BUTTON

1" R

5"

SIDE
MAKE 2

8$\frac{1}{2}$"

STOP

$\frac{1}{2}$"

8$\frac{1}{4}$"

6$\frac{1}{4}$"

ROOF

2"

6$\frac{1}{4}$"

5"

5"

BOTTOM

ROUNDED

BUTT JOINTS

FRONT

BOTTOM IS HINGED ON NAILS
AND HELD AGAINST A STOP BY
MEANS OF A TURN BUTTON. ALL
MATERIAL IS 1/2 INCH EXCEPT
ROUNDED TOP PIECE. SCREW
EYES SHOULD EXTEND DOWN IN-
FLAT ROOF. PAINT TO SUIT.

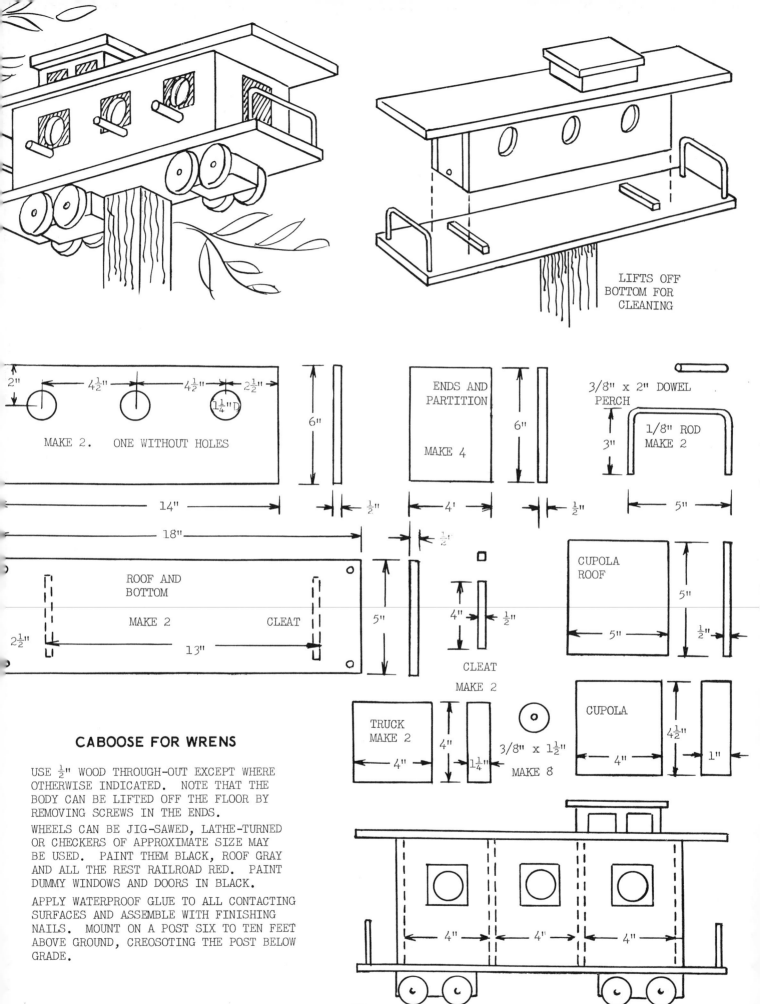

LIFTS OFF
BOTTOM FOR
CLEANING

2" 4½" 4½" 2½"

1¼" D

6"

MAKE 2.   ONE WITHOUT HOLES

14"

½"

18"

½"

ROOF AND
BOTTOM

MAKE 2   CLEAT

2½"

13"

5"

ENDS AND
PARTITION

MAKE 4

6"

4'

½"

4"

½"

CLEAT

MAKE 2

4"

½"

TRUCK
MAKE 2

4"

4"

1¼"

3/8" x 1½"

MAKE 8

3/8" x 2" DOWEL
PERCH

3"

1/8" ROD
MAKE 2

5"

CUPOLA
ROOF

5"

5"

½"

CUPOLA

4"

4½"

1"

CABOOSE FOR WRENS

USE ½" WOOD THROUGH-OUT EXCEPT WHERE
OTHERWISE INDICATED. NOTE THAT THE
BODY CAN BE LIFTED OFF THE FLOOR BY
REMOVING SCREWS IN THE ENDS.

WHEELS CAN BE JIG-SAWED, LATHE-TURNED
OR CHECKERS OF APPROXIMATE SIZE MAY
BE USED. PAINT THEM BLACK, ROOF GRAY
AND ALL THE REST RAILROAD RED. PAINT
DUMMY WINDOWS AND DOORS IN BLACK.

APPLY WATERPROOF GLUE TO ALL CONTACTING
SURFACES AND ASSEMBLE WITH FINISHING
NAILS. MOUNT ON A POST SIX TO TEN FEET
ABOVE GROUND, CREOSOTING THE POST BELOW
GRADE.

4"   4"   4"

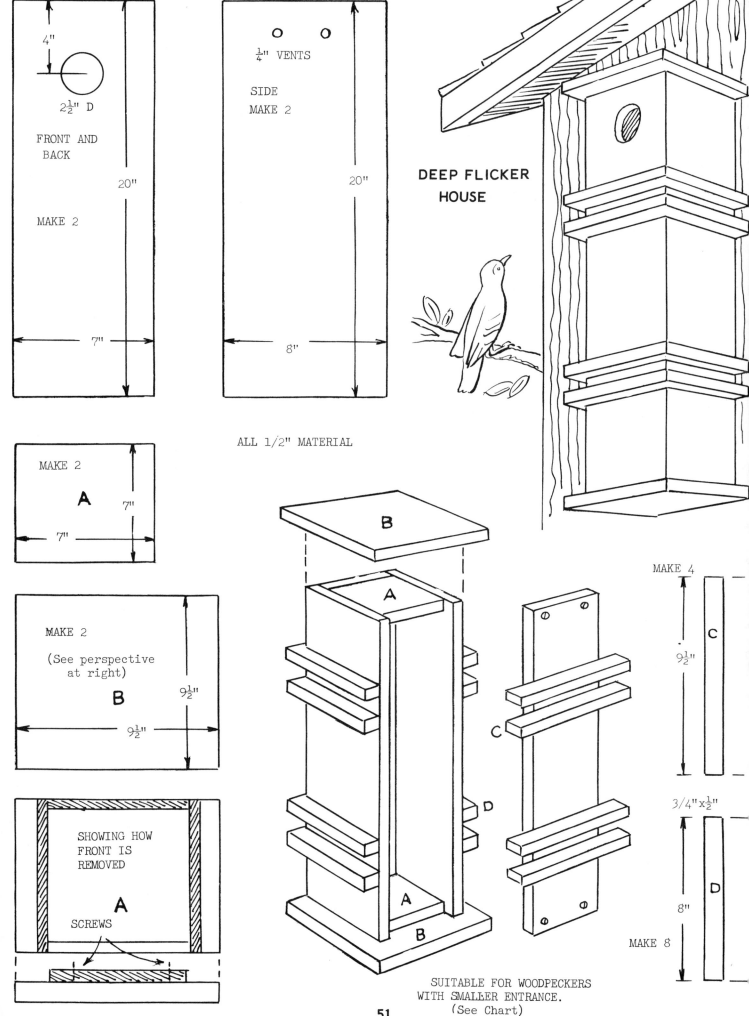

4"

2½" D

FRONT AND
BACK

MAKE 2

20"

7"

¼" VENTS

SIDE
MAKE 2

20"

8"

ALL 1/2" MATERIAL

DEEP FLICKER
HOUSE

MAKE 2

A

7"

7"

MAKE 2

(See perspective
at right)

B

9½"

9½"

SHOWING HOW
FRONT IS
REMOVED

A

SCREWS

B

A

A

B

C

D

MAKE 4

C

9½"

3/4"x½"

D

8"

MAKE 8

SUITABLE FOR WOODPECKERS
WITH SMALLER ENTRANCE.
(See Chart)

51

HOTEL MARTIN
(58 Rooms)

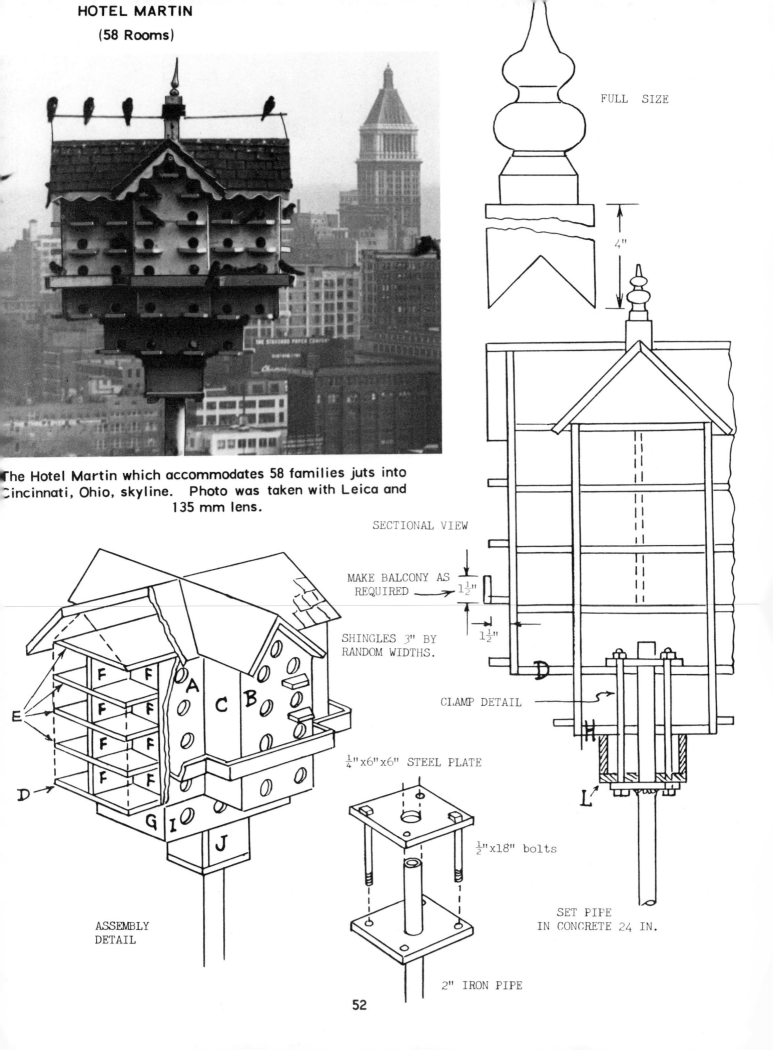

The Hotel Martin which accommodates 58 families juts into Cincinnati, Ohio, skyline. Photo was taken with Leica and 135 mm lens.

FULL SIZE

4"

SECTIONAL VIEW

MAKE BALCONY AS REQUIRED $1\frac{1}{2}$"

$1\frac{1}{2}$"

D

SHINGLES 3" BY RANDOM WIDTHS.

CLAMP DETAIL

L

$\frac{1}{4}$"x6"x6" STEEL PLATE

E

D

F F F
F F F
F F F
F F F

A
C B

G I
J

$\frac{1}{2}$"x18" bolts

SET PIPE
IN CONCRETE 24 IN.

ASSEMBLY
DETAIL

2" IRON PIPE

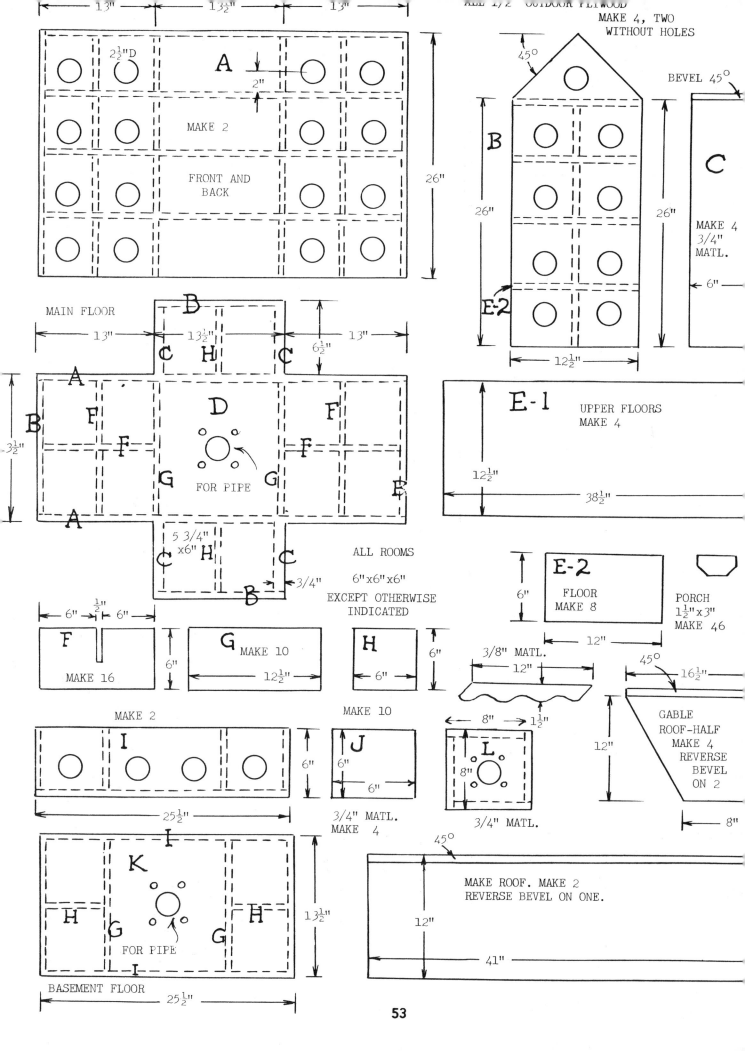

ALL 1/2" OUTDOOR PLYWOOD

MAKE 4, TWO
WITHOUT HOLES

45°

BEVEL 45°

13"   13½"   13"

2½"D

A

2"

26"

MAKE 2

FRONT AND
BACK

B

26"

26"

E-2

12½"

C

MAKE 4
3/4"
MATL.

6"

MAIN FLOOR

13"   13½"   13"

6½"

B

C   H   C

A

B

F   F

3½"

F   D   F

FOR PIPE

G   G

A

E

C   H   C

5 3/4"
x6"

B   3/4"

ALL ROOMS

6"x6"x6"

EXCEPT OTHERWISE
INDICATED

E-1   UPPER FLOORS
MAKE 4

12½"

38½"

½"

6"   6"

F

MAKE 16

6"

G   MAKE 10

12½"

H

6"

6"

E-2
FLOOR
MAKE 8

6"

12"

PORCH
1½"x3"
MAKE 46

MAKE 2

MAKE 10

3/8" MATL.

12"

1½"

8"

45°

16½"

GABLE
ROOF-HALF
MAKE 4
REVERSE
BEVEL
ON 2

I

6"

J

6"

6"

L

8"

8"

12"

25½"

3/4" MATL.
MAKE 4

3/4" MATL.

8"

45°

I

K

13½"

H   H

G   G

FOR PIPE

I

MAKE ROOF. MAKE 2
REVERSE BEVEL ON ONE.

12"

41"

BASEMENT FLOOR

25½"

53

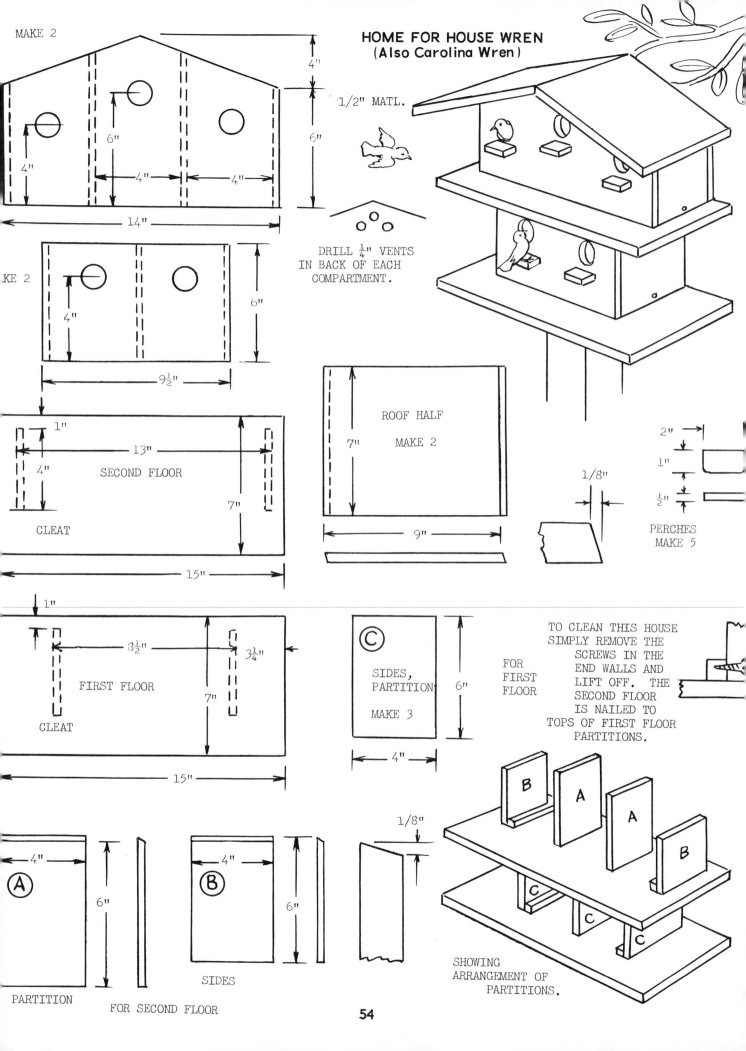

MAKE 2

4"

6"

1/2" MATL.

HOME FOR HOUSE WREN
(Also Carolina Wren)

6"

4"

4"

4"

4"

4"

14"

DRILL ¼" VENTS
IN BACK OF EACH
COMPARTMENT.

KE 2

4"

6"

9½"

1"

13"

4"

SECOND FLOOR

7"

CLEAT

15"

ROOF HALF

MAKE 2

7"

9"

1/8"

2"

1"

½"

PERCHES
MAKE 5

1"

8½"

3¼"

FIRST FLOOR

7"

CLEAT

15"

Ⓒ

SIDES,
PARTITION

MAKE 3

6"

4"

FOR
FIRST
FLOOR

TO CLEAN THIS HOUSE
SIMPLY REMOVE THE
SCREWS IN THE
END WALLS AND
LIFT OFF. THE
SECOND FLOOR
IS NAILED TO
TOPS OF FIRST FLOOR
PARTITIONS.

1/8"

Ⓐ

4"

6"

Ⓑ

4"

6"

1/8"

B A A B

C C C

PARTITION

FOR SECOND FLOOR

SIDES

SHOWING
ARRANGEMENT OF
PARTITIONS.

54

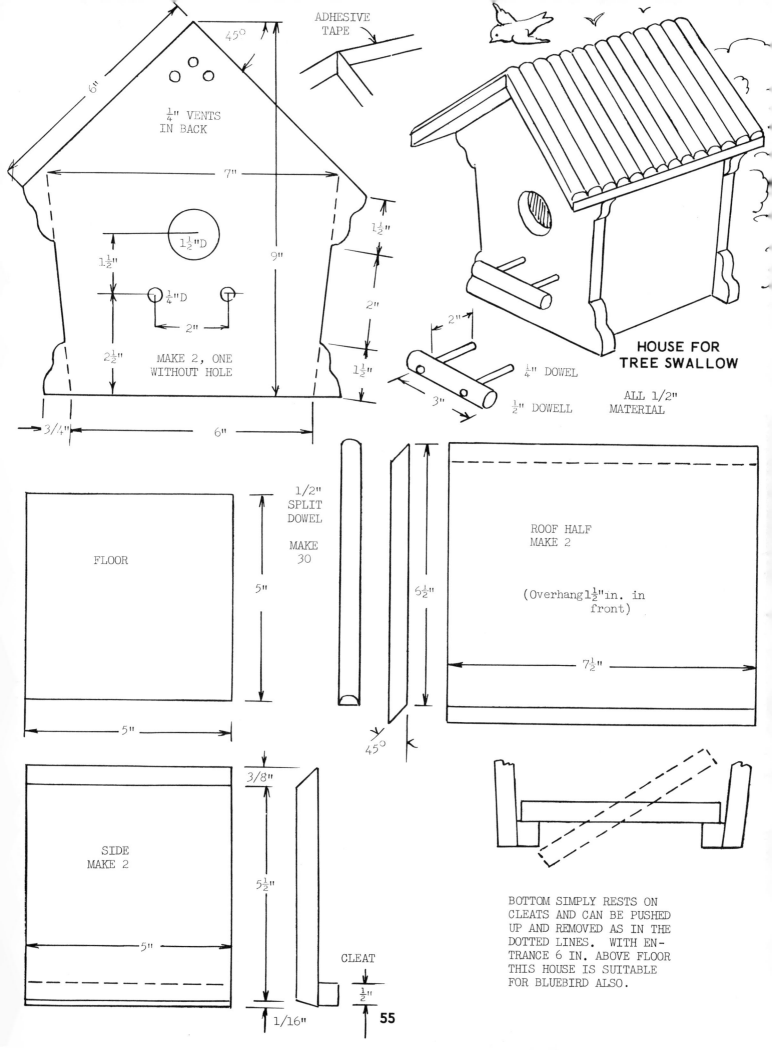

45°

ADHESIVE
TAPE

$\frac{1}{4}$" VENTS
IN BACK

6"

7"

9"

$1\frac{1}{2}$"D

$1\frac{1}{2}$"

$\frac{1}{4}$"D

2"

2"

$2\frac{1}{2}$"

$1\frac{1}{2}$"

MAKE 2, ONE
WITHOUT HOLE

3/4"

6"

HOUSE FOR
TREE SWALLOW

2"

$\frac{1}{4}$" DOWEL

3"

$\frac{1}{2}$" DOWELL

ALL 1/2"
MATERIAL

FLOOR

5"

5"

1/2"
SPLIT
DOWEL

MAKE
30

$6\frac{1}{2}$"

45°

ROOF HALF
MAKE 2

(Overhang $1\frac{1}{2}$"in. in
front)

$7\frac{1}{2}$"

SIDE
MAKE 2

5"

3/8"

$5\frac{1}{2}$"

CLEAT

$\frac{1}{2}$"

1/16"

BOTTOM SIMPLY RESTS ON
CLEATS AND CAN BE PUSHED
UP AND REMOVED AS IN THE
DOTTED LINES. WITH EN-
TRANCE 6 IN. ABOVE FLOOR
THIS HOUSE IS SUITABLE
FOR BLUEBIRD ALSO.

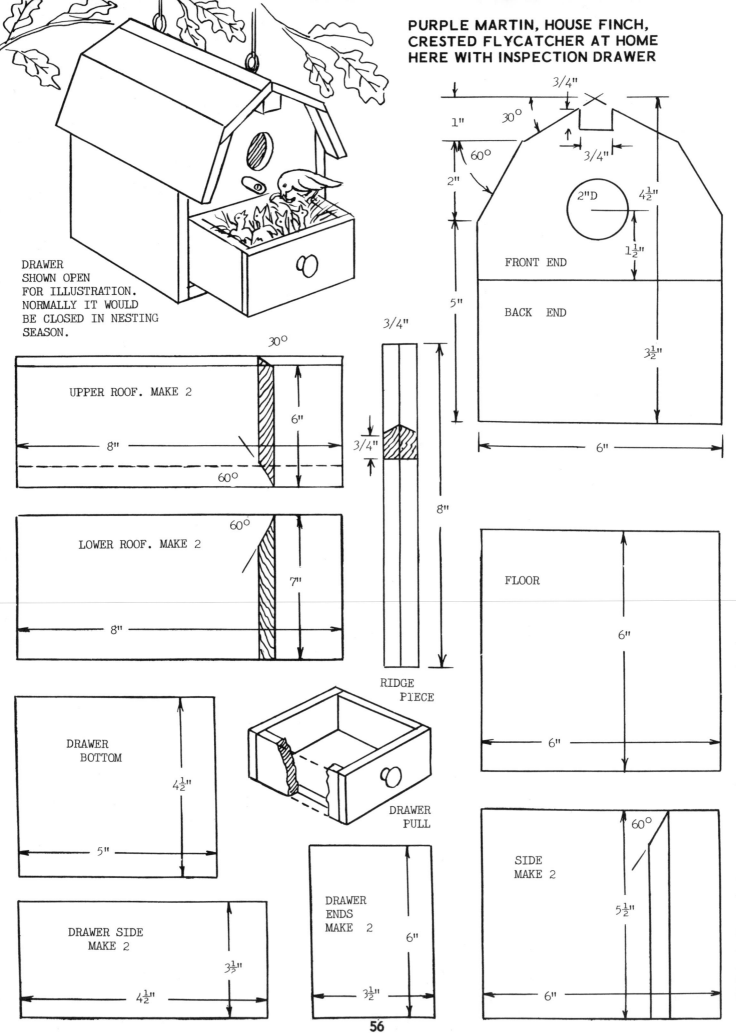

PURPLE MARTIN, HOUSE FINCH,
CRESTED FLYCATCHER AT HOME
HERE WITH INSPECTION DRAWER

DRAWER
SHOWN OPEN
FOR ILLUSTRATION.
NORMALLY IT WOULD
BE CLOSED IN NESTING
SEASON.

FRONT END

BACK END

2"D

UPPER ROOF. MAKE 2

LOWER ROOF. MAKE 2

RIDGE
PIECE

FLOOR

DRAWER
BOTTOM

DRAWER
PULL

DRAWER SIDE
MAKE 2

DRAWER
ENDS
MAKE 2

SIDE
MAKE 2

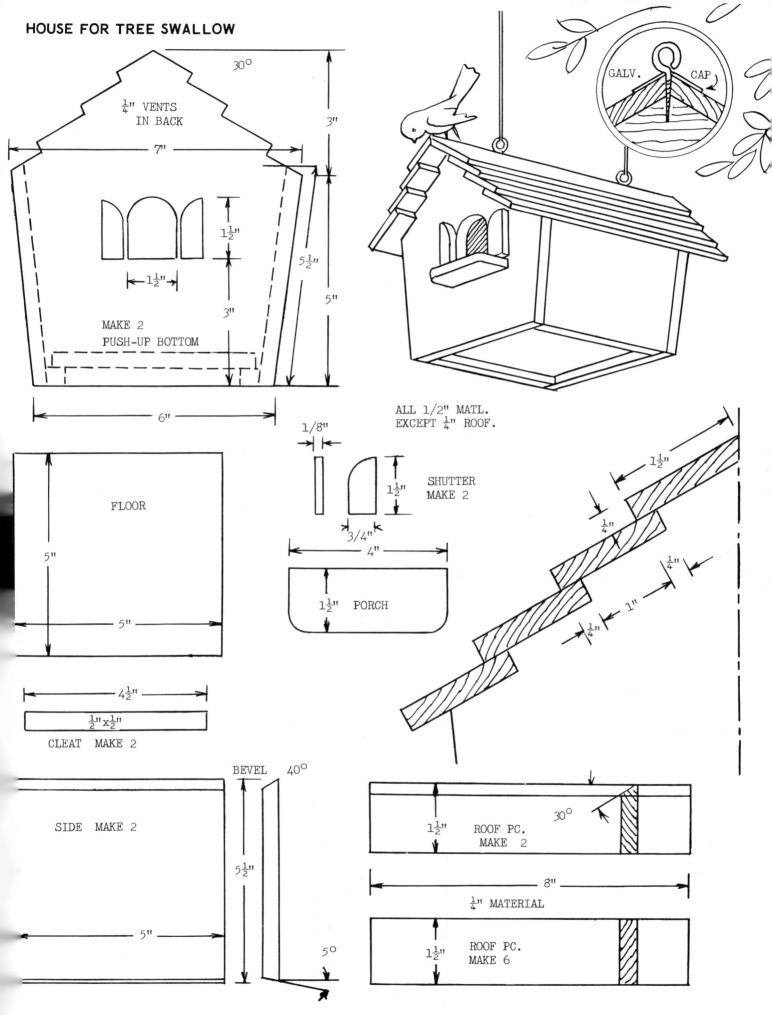

30°

¼" VENTS IN BACK

3"

7"

1½"

1½"

5½"

3"

5"

MAKE 2
PUSH-UP BOTTOM

6"

GALV.   CAP

ALL 1/2" MATL.
EXCEPT ¼" ROOF.

1/8"

1½"

SHUTTER
MAKE 2

3/4"

4"

1½"   PORCH

FLOOR

5"

5"

4½"

½" x ½"

CLEAT MAKE 2

BEVEL   40°

SIDE   MAKE 2

5½"

5"

5°

1½"

¼"

¼"

1"

¼"

1½"   ROOF PC.
MAKE 2

30°

8"

¼" MATERIAL

1½"   ROOF PC.
MAKE 6

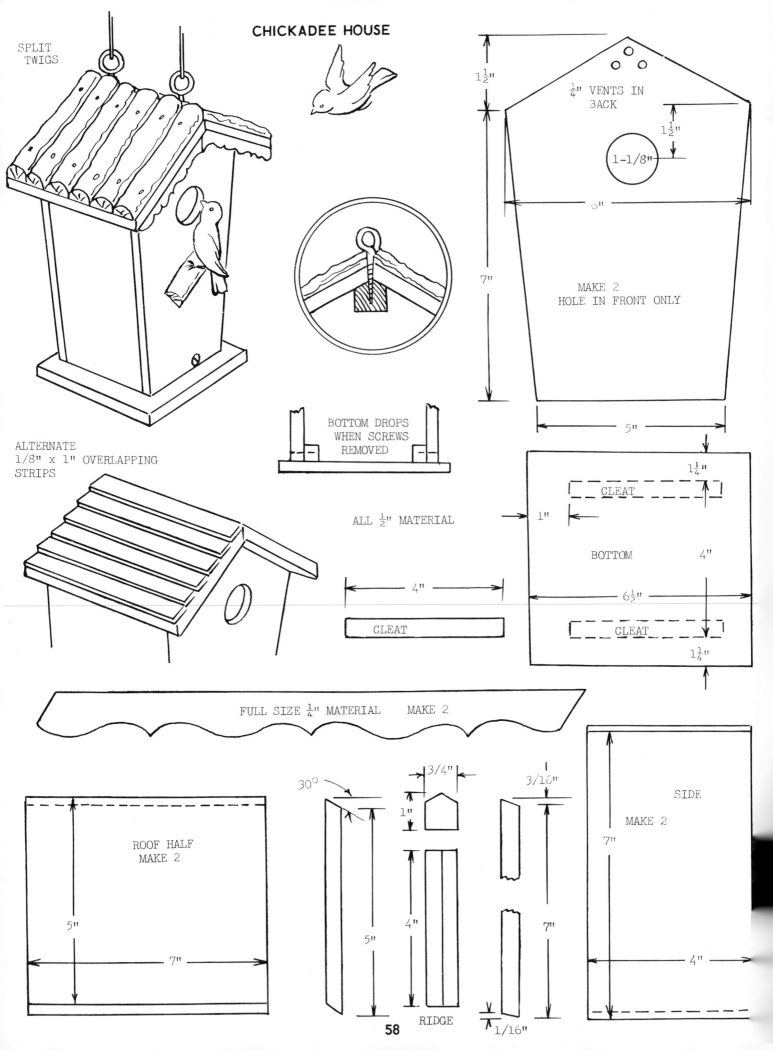

CHICKADEE HOUSE

SPLIT TWIGS

ALTERNATE 1/8" x 1" OVERLAPPING STRIPS

¼" VENTS IN BACK

1½"

1½"

1-1/8"

5"

7"

MAKE 2
HOLE IN FRONT ONLY

BOTTOM DROPS WHEN SCREWS REMOVED

ALL ½" MATERIAL

CLEAT

4"

CLEAT

1¼"

BOTTOM

1"

4"

6½"

CLEAT

1¼"

FULL SIZE ¼" MATERIAL   MAKE 2

ROOF HALF
MAKE 2

5"

7"

30°

3/4"

1"

5"

4"

3/16"

7"

SIDE
MAKE 2

7"

4"

RIDGE

1/16"

58

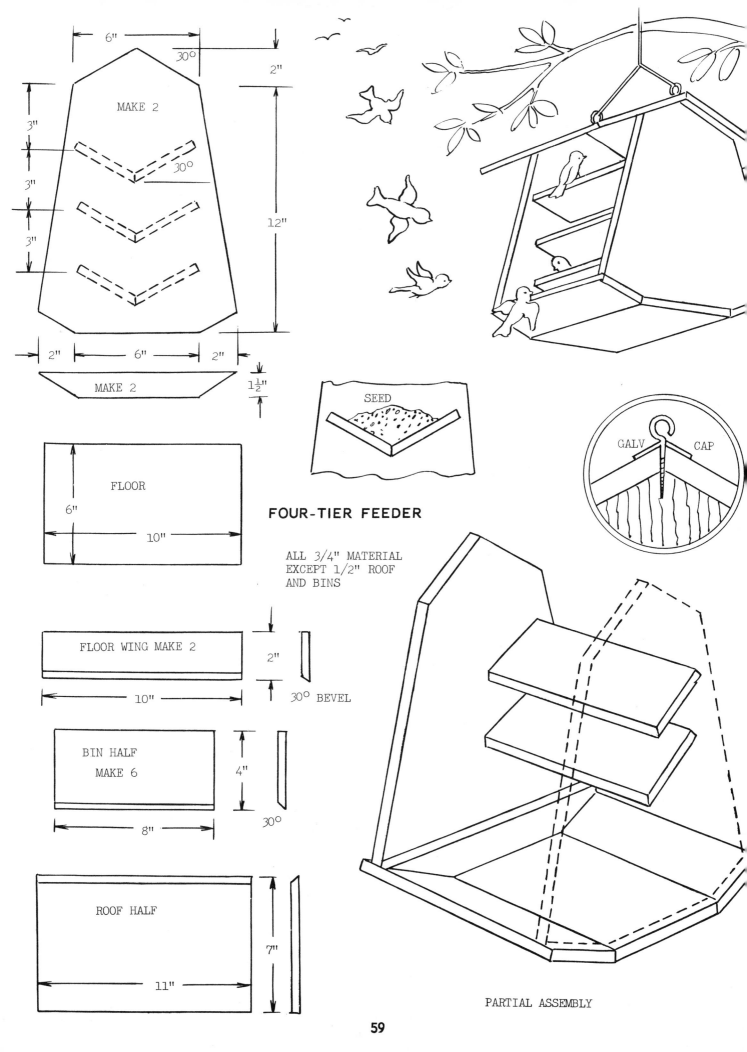

6"

30°

2"

MAKE 2

3"

3"

30°

3"

3"

12"

2" 6" 2"

MAKE 2

1½"

FLOOR

6"

10"

SEED

FOUR-TIER FEEDER

ALL 3/4" MATERIAL
EXCEPT 1/2" ROOF
AND BINS

GALV CAP

FLOOR WING MAKE 2

2"

10"

30° BEVEL

BIN HALF

MAKE 6

4"

8"

30°

ROOF HALF

7"

11"

PARTIAL ASSEMBLY

59

WIND VANE FEEDER
(Revolves With Back To Wind)

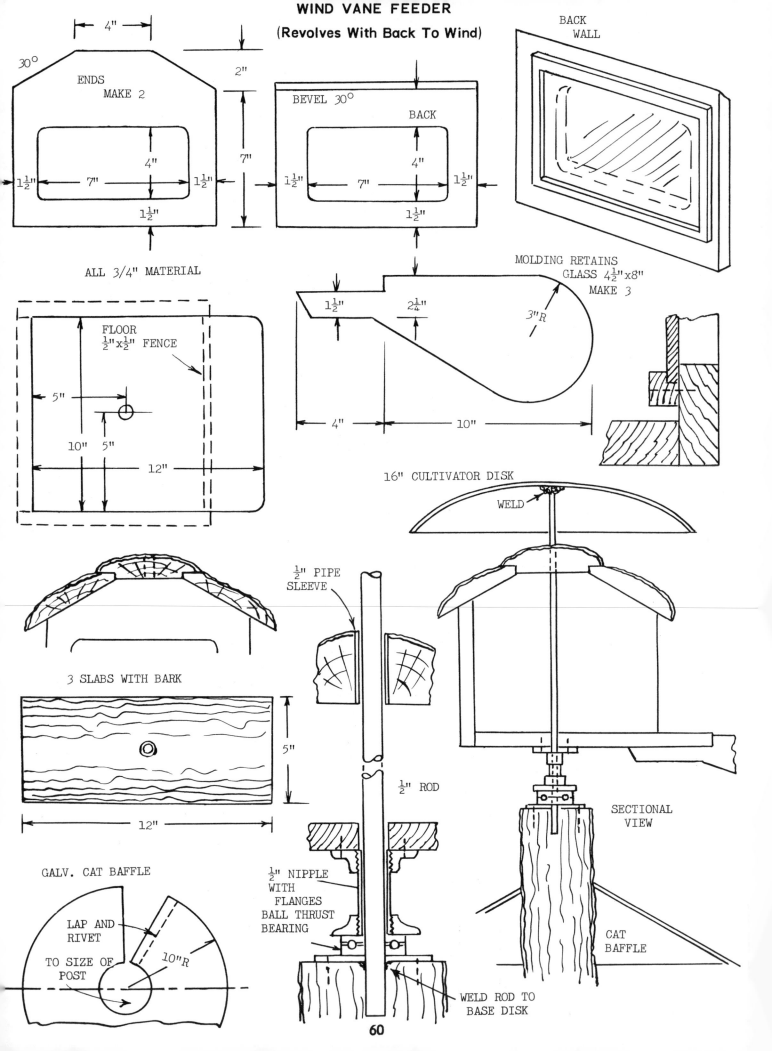

4"

30°

ENDS
MAKE 2

2"

7"

4"

1½"   7"   1½"

1½"

ALL 3/4" MATERIAL

BEVEL 30°

BACK

4"

1½"   7"   1½"

1½"

BACK WALL

MOLDING RETAINS
GLASS 4½"x8"
MAKE 3

3"R

1½"   2¼"

4"   10"

FLOOR
½"x½" FENCE

5"

10"   5"

12"

16" CULTIVATOR DISK

WELD

½" PIPE
SLEEVE

½" ROD

SECTIONAL
VIEW

3 SLABS WITH BARK

5"

12"

GALV. CAT BAFFLE

LAP AND
RIVET

TO SIZE OF
POST

10"R

½" NIPPLE
WITH
FLANGES
BALL THRUST
BEARING

CAT
BAFFLE

WELD ROD TO
BASE DISK

BIRD CHAPEL

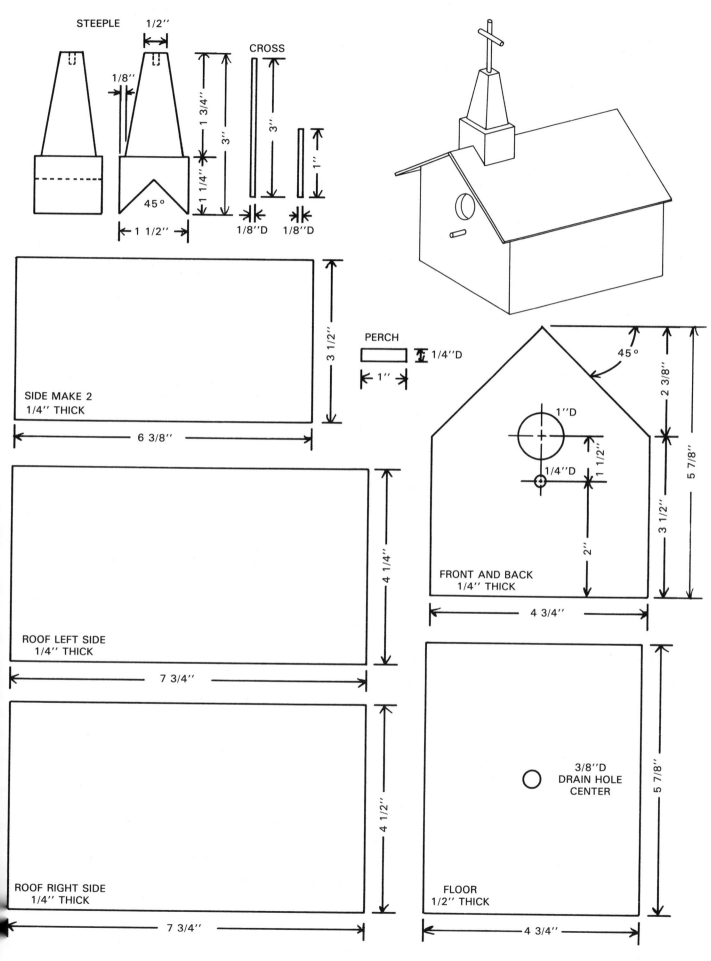

STEEPLE 1/2''

1/8''

CROSS

1 3/4''

3''

3''

1''

1 1/4''

45°

1 1/2''

1/8''D   1/8''D

SIDE MAKE 2
1/4'' THICK

3 1/2''

6 3/8''

PERCH

1/4''D

1''

ROOF LEFT SIDE
1/4'' THICK

4 1/4''

7 3/4''

FRONT AND BACK
1/4'' THICK

45°

2 3/8''

5 7/8''

3 1/2''

1''D

1/4''D

1 1/2''

2''

4 3/4''

ROOF RIGHT SIDE
1/4'' THICK

4 1/2''

7 3/4''

FLOOR
1/2'' THICK

3/8''D
DRAIN HOLE
CENTER

5 7/8''

4 3/4''

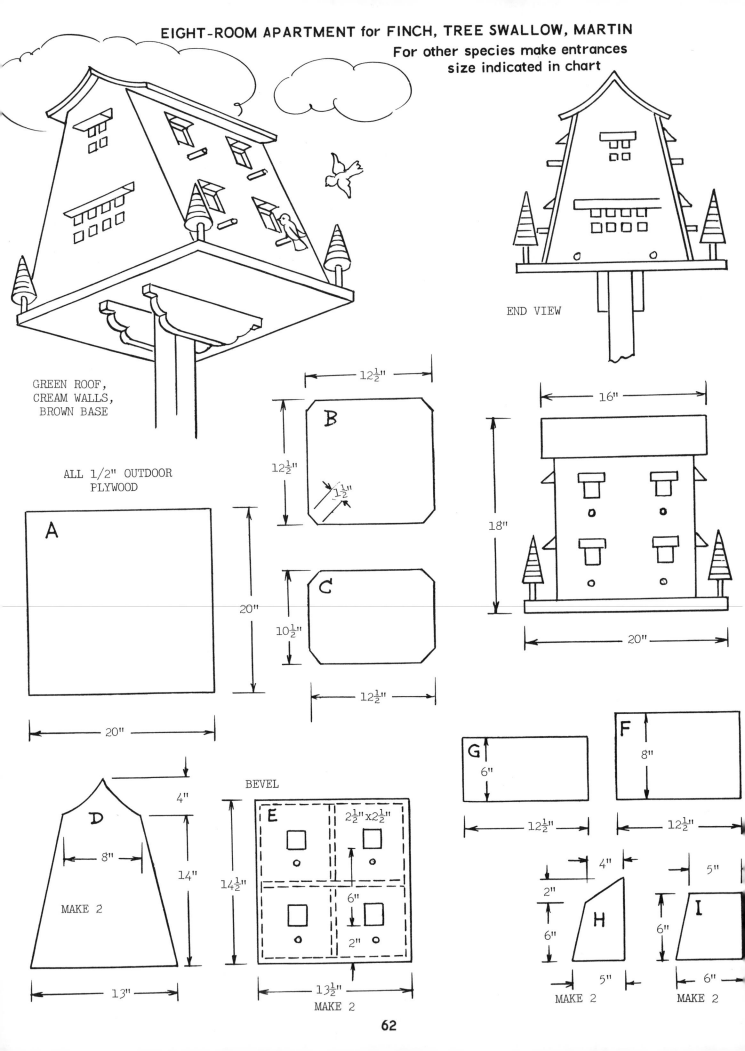

GREEN ROOF,
CREAM WALLS,
BROWN BASE

END VIEW

ALL 1/2" OUTDOOR PLYWOOD

A — 20" × 20"

B — 12½" × 12½", 1½"

C — 10½" × 12½"

D — MAKE 2 — 4", 8", 14", 13"

BEVEL

E — 2½" × 2½", 6", 2" — 14½" — 13½" — MAKE 2

G — 6" × 12½"

F — 8" × 12½"

H — 2", 6", 4", 5" — MAKE 2

I — 5", 6", 6" — MAKE 2

16" — 18" — 20"

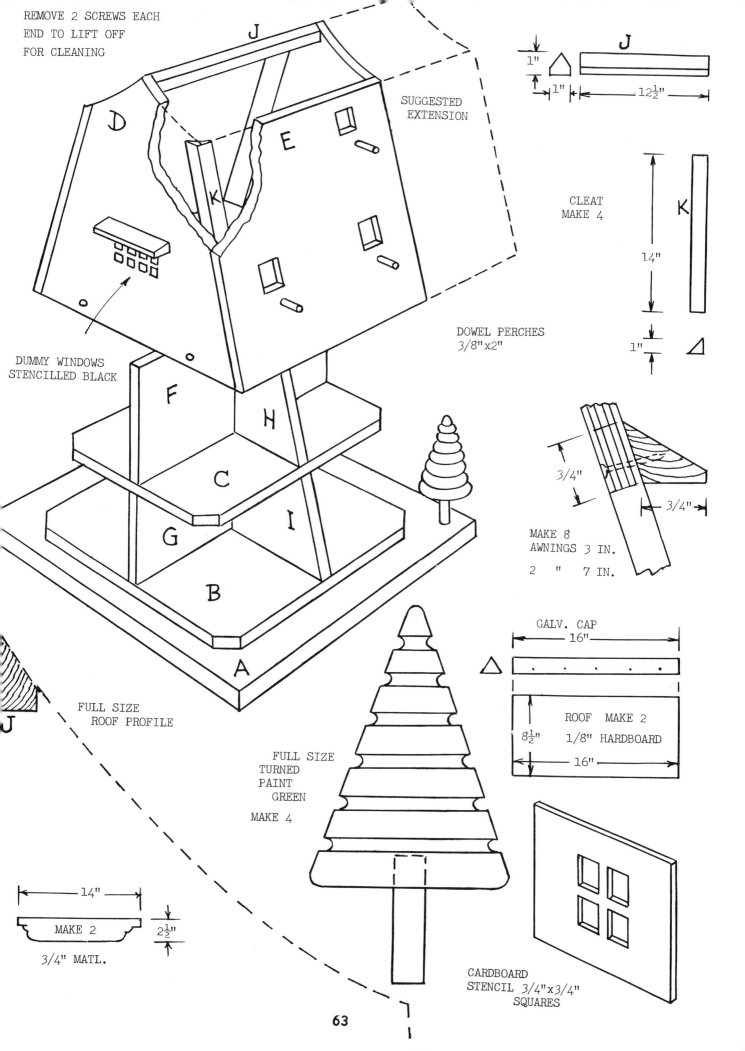

REMOVE 2 SCREWS EACH
END TO LIFT OFF
FOR CLEANING

D

J

E

K

SUGGESTED
EXTENSION

J

1"

1"

12½"

CLEAT
MAKE 4

K

14"

1"

DOWEL PERCHES
3/8"x2"

DUMMY WINDOWS
STENCILLED BLACK

F

H

C

G

I

B

A

3/4"

3/4"

MAKE 8
AWNINGS 3 IN.

2 " 7 IN.

GALV. CAP
16"

ROOF   MAKE 2
1/8" HARDBOARD

8½"

16"

J

FULL SIZE
ROOF PROFILE

FULL SIZE
TURNED
PAINT
GREEN

MAKE 4

14"

MAKE 2

2½"

3/4" MATL.

CARDBOARD
STENCIL 3/4"x3/4"
SQUARES

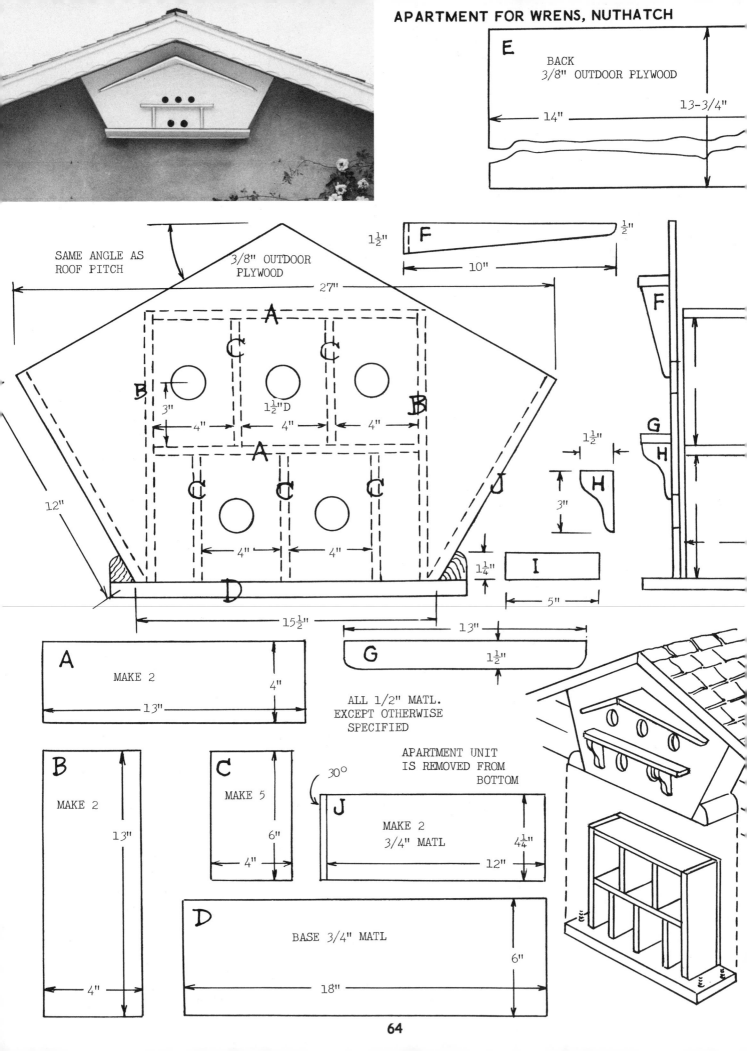

E

BACK
3/8" OUTDOOR PLYWOOD

14"

13-3/4"

SAME ANGLE AS
ROOF PITCH

3/8" OUTDOOR
PLYWOOD

27"

F

1½"

½"

10"

A

C   C

B   B

3"

1½"D

4"   4"   4"

A

12"

C   C   C

4"   4"

J

1½"

H

3"

I

1¼"

5"

D

15½"

13"

G

1½"

A

MAKE 2

4"

13"

ALL 1/2" MATL.
EXCEPT OTHERWISE
SPECIFIED

APARTMENT UNIT
IS REMOVED FROM
BOTTOM

B

MAKE 2

13"

4"

C

MAKE 5

6"

4"

30°

J

MAKE 2
3/4" MATL

4¼"

12"

D

BASE 3/4" MATL

6"

18"

64

FOR THE CRESTED FLYCATCHER

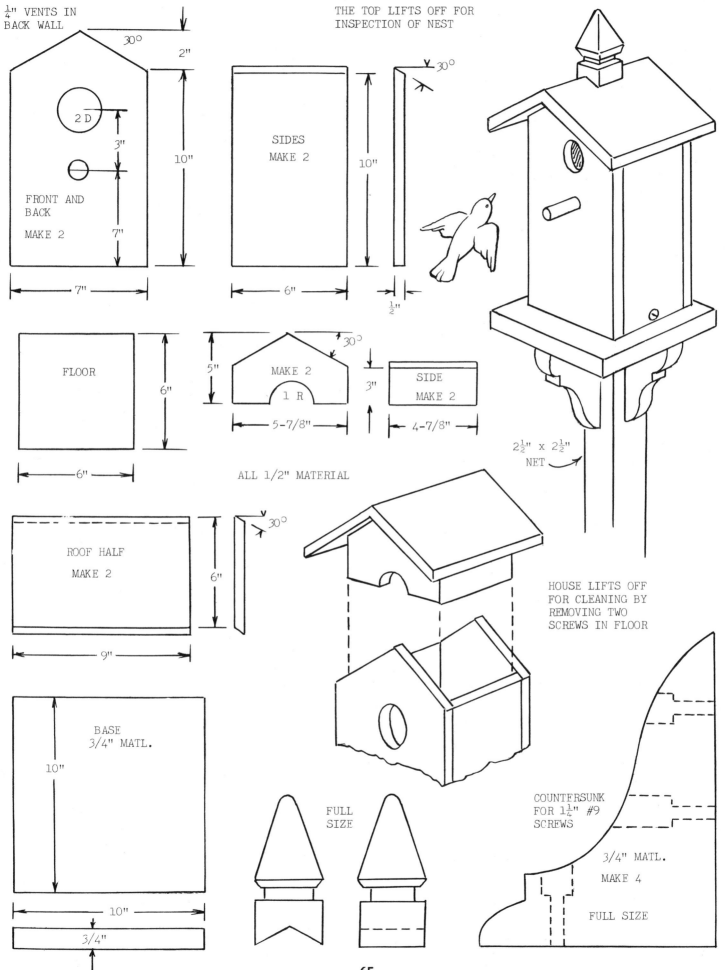

¼" VENTS IN
BACK WALL

30°

2"

2 D

3"

10"

FRONT AND
BACK

MAKE 2

7"

7"

THE TOP LIFTS OFF FOR
INSPECTION OF NEST

SIDES
MAKE 2

10"

30°

6"

½

FLOOR

6"

6"

5"

MAKE 2

1 R

5-7/8"

30°

3"

SIDE
MAKE 2

4-7/8"

ALL 1/2" MATERIAL

2½" x 2½"
NET

ROOF HALF

MAKE 2

6"

30°

9"

HOUSE LIFTS OFF
FOR CLEANING BY
REMOVING TWO
SCREWS IN FLOOR

BASE
3/4" MATL.

10"

10"

3/4"

FULL
SIZE

COUNTERSUNK
FOR 1¼" #9
SCREWS

3/4" MATL.

MAKE 4

FULL SIZE

65

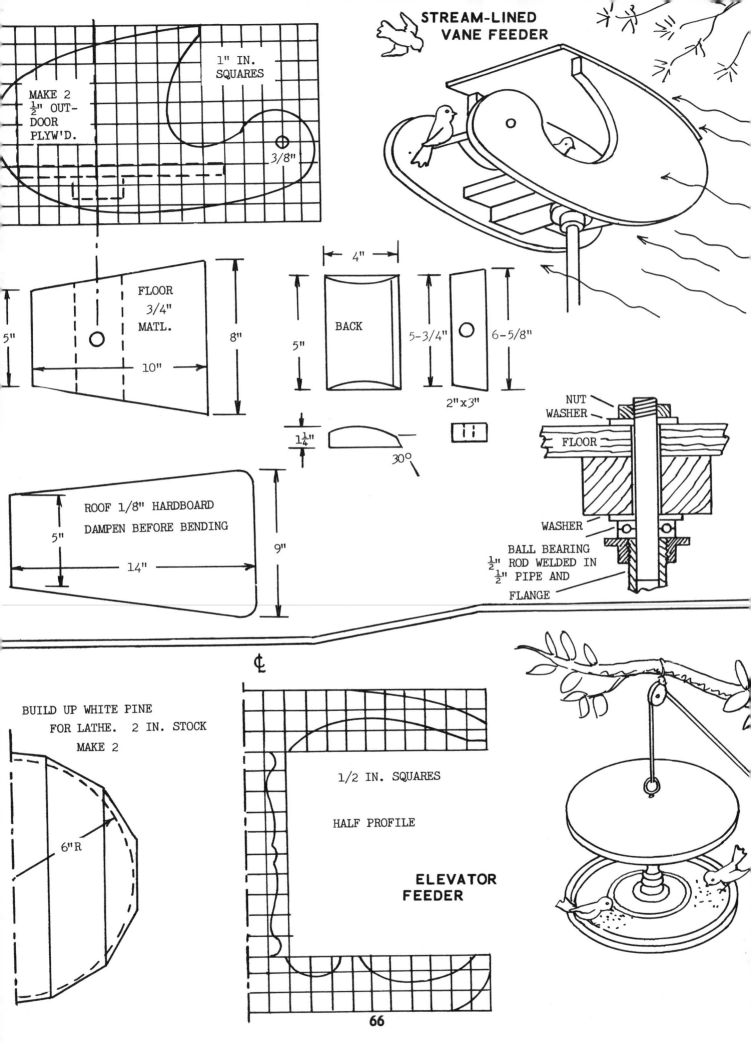

STREAM-LINED
VANE FEEDER

1" IN.
SQUARES

MAKE 2
½" OUT-
DOOR
PLYW'D.

3/8"

FLOOR
3/4"
MATL.

5"   8"

10"

4"

BACK

5"   5-3/4"   6-5/8"

2"x3"

1¼"

30°

NUT
WASHER

FLOOR

WASHER

BALL BEARING
½" ROD WELDED IN
½" PIPE AND
FLANGE

ROOF 1/8" HARDBOARD
DAMPEN BEFORE BENDING

5"   9"

14"

BUILD UP WHITE PINE
FOR LATHE. 2 IN. STOCK
MAKE 2

6"R

₵

1/2 IN. SQUARES

HALF PROFILE

ELEVATOR
FEEDER

66

JAPANESE COTTAGE FOR PURPLE MARTIN

A VERY PICTURESQUE HOUSE IN ORIENTAL STYLE WITH GOLD SPIRES AND CURVED ROOF BEAMS, THE ROOF ITSELF GREEN AND THE WALLS IN NATURAL GRAIN. WINDOWS CAN BE MARKED ON THE RAW WOOD WITH A SOFT BLACK PENCIL.

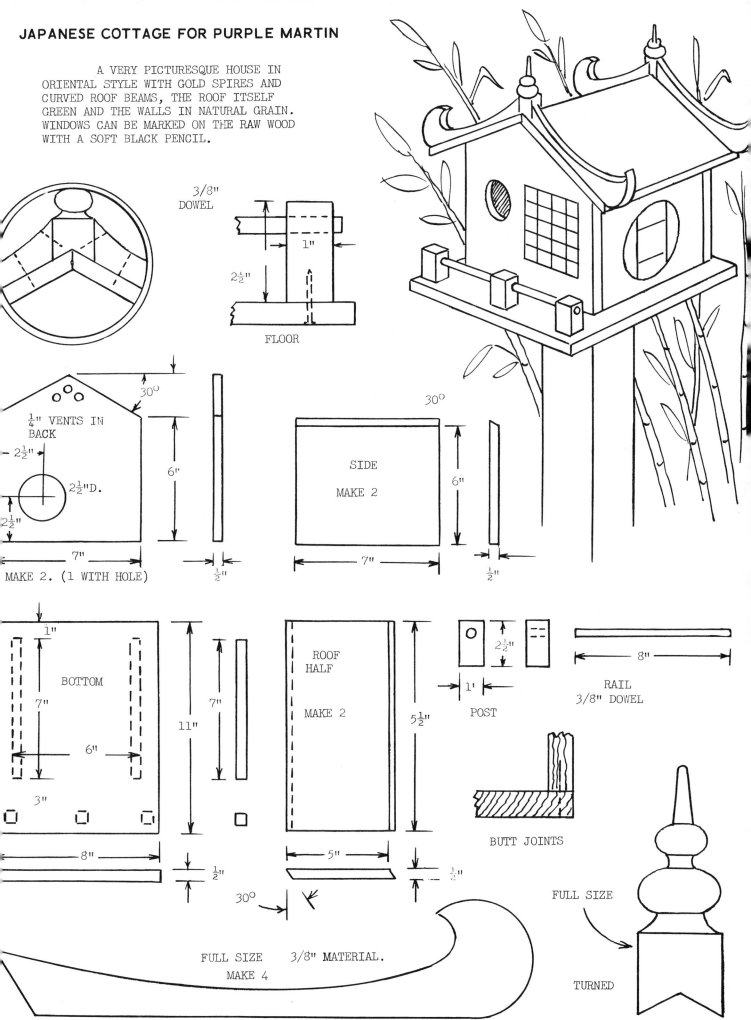

3/8" DOWEL

FLOOR

1"

2½"

30°

¼" VENTS IN BACK

2½"

2½"D.

2½"

6"

7"

½"

MAKE 2. (1 WITH HOLE)

30°

SIDE
MAKE 2

6"

7"

½"

1"

BOTTOM

7"

6"

3"

8"

½"

11"

7"

ROOF
HALF

MAKE 2

5½"

5"

½"

30°

FULL SIZE   3/8" MATERIAL.
MAKE 4

2½"

1'

POST

8"

RAIL
3/8" DOWEL

BUTT JOINTS

FULL SIZE

TURNED

WOOD BIRD BATH WITH FOUNTAIN

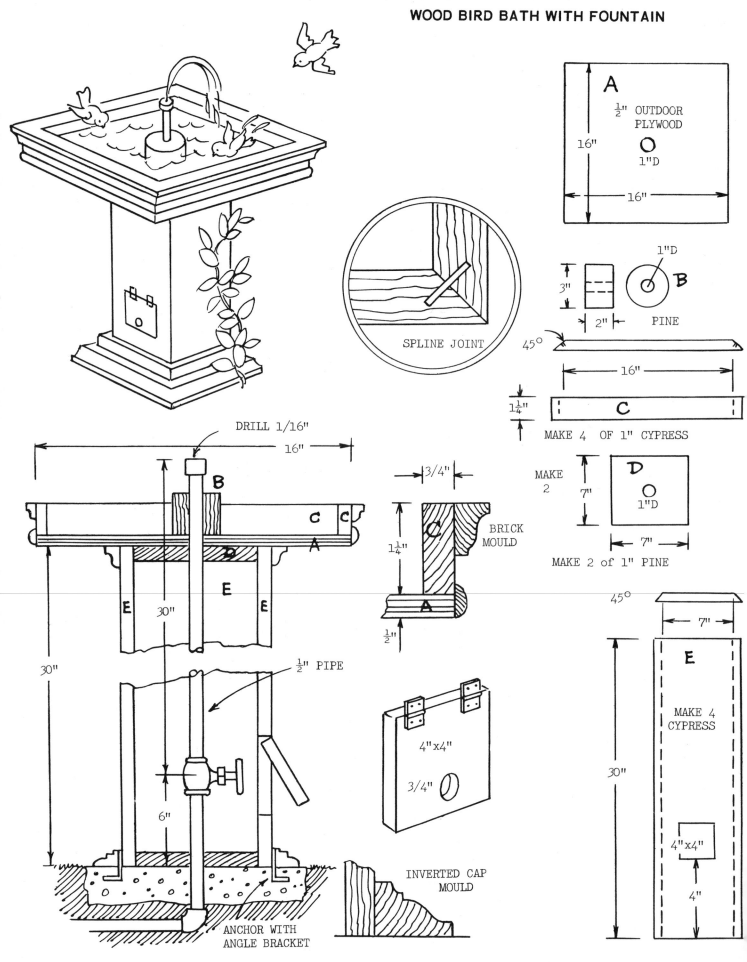

A
½" OUTDOOR PLYWOOD
16"
16"
1"D

B
3"
2"
1"D
PINE

45°
16"
1¼"
C
MAKE 4 OF 1" CYPRESS

SPLINE JOINT

MAKE 2
D
7"
1"D
7"
MAKE 2 of 1" PINE

DRILL 1/16"
16"
B
C **C**
A
E **E** **E**
30"
30"
6"
½" PIPE
ANCHOR WITH ANGLE BRACKET

3/4"
C
BRICK MOULD
1¼"
A
½"

4"x4"
3/4"

INVERTED CAP MOULD

45°
7"
E
MAKE 4 CYPRESS
30"
4"x4"
4"

APPLY MARINE GLUE TO ALL CONTACTING SURFACES. DO NOT MAKE BASIN DEEPER
THAN 1¼" AS BIRDS FEAR DEEPER WATER. REDWOOD MAY BE USED INSTEAD OF CYPRESS.

68

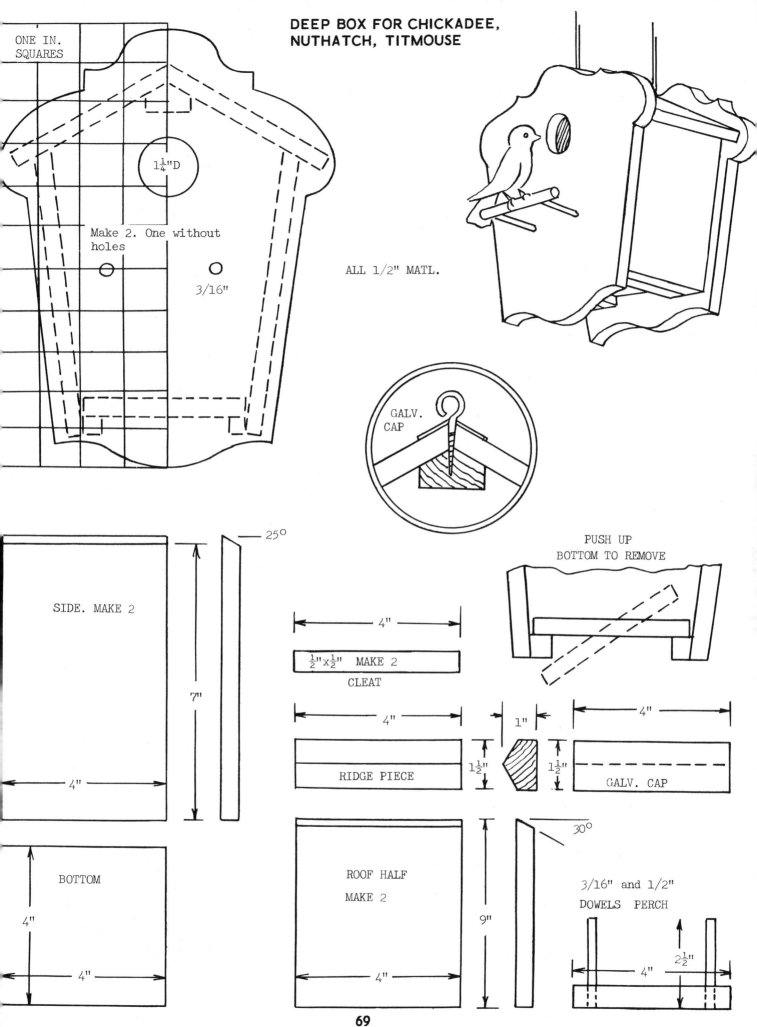

ONE IN.
SQUARES

DEEP BOX FOR CHICKADEE,
NUTHATCH, TITMOUSE

$1\frac{1}{4}$"D

Make 2. One without
holes

3/16"

ALL 1/2" MATL.

GALV.
CAP

25°

SIDE. MAKE 2

7"

4"

BOTTOM

4"

4"

4"

$\frac{1}{2}$"x$\frac{1}{2}$" MAKE 2

CLEAT

4"

RIDGE PIECE

1"

$1\frac{1}{2}$"

$1\frac{1}{2}$"

4"

GALV. CAP

PUSH UP
BOTTOM TO REMOVE

ROOF HALF

MAKE 2

9"

4"

30°

3/16" and 1/2"

DOWELS PERCH

$2\frac{1}{2}$"

4"

69

TOPS OF EACH
STORY UNSCREW
FOR CLEANING

ALL 1/2 IN.
OUTDOOR PLYWOOD

STAGGER PARTITIONS
FOR EASIER NAILING

20"

36"

16"

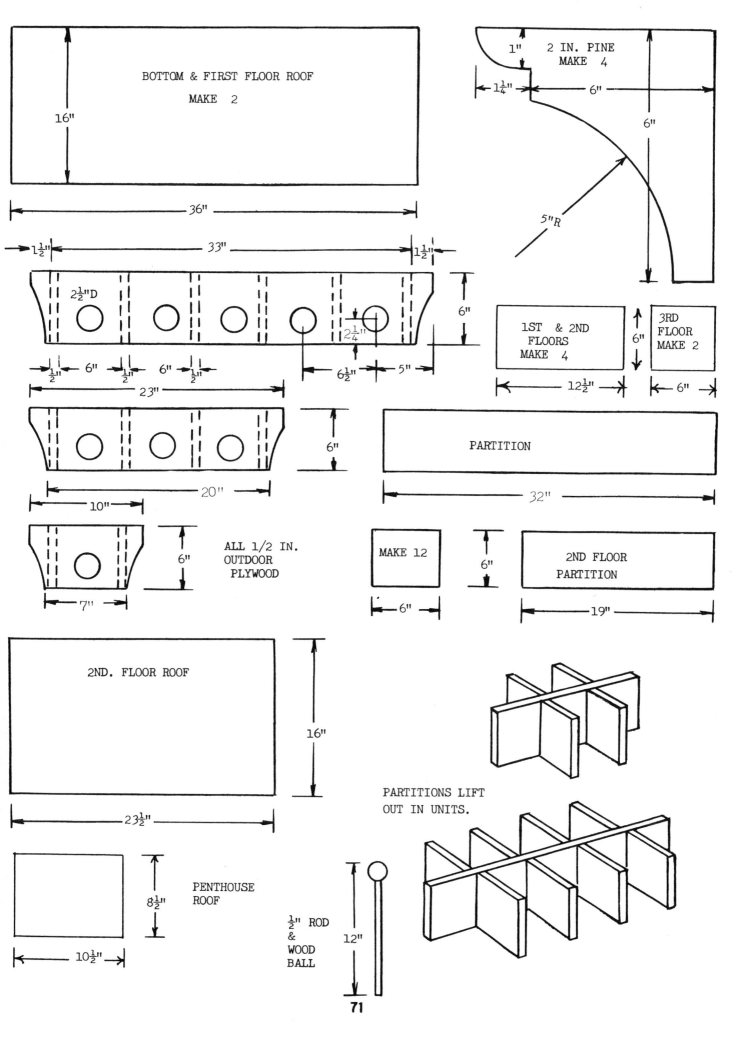

BOTTOM & FIRST FLOOR ROOF
MAKE 2

16"

36"

2 IN. PINE
MAKE 4

1"

1¼"

6"

6"

5"R

1½"

33"

1½"

2½"D

6"

2¼"

½"

6"

½"

6"

½"

23"

6½"

5"

1ST & 2ND
FLOORS
MAKE 4

3RD
FLOOR
MAKE 2

6"

12½"

6"

6"

PARTITION

32"

20"

10"

MAKE 12

6"

2ND FLOOR
PARTITION

6"

19"

ALL 1/2 IN.
OUTDOOR
PLYWOOD

6"

7"

2ND. FLOOR ROOF

16"

23½"

PARTITIONS LIFT
OUT IN UNITS.

PENTHOUSE
ROOF

8½"

10½"

½" ROD
&
WOOD
BALL

12"

71

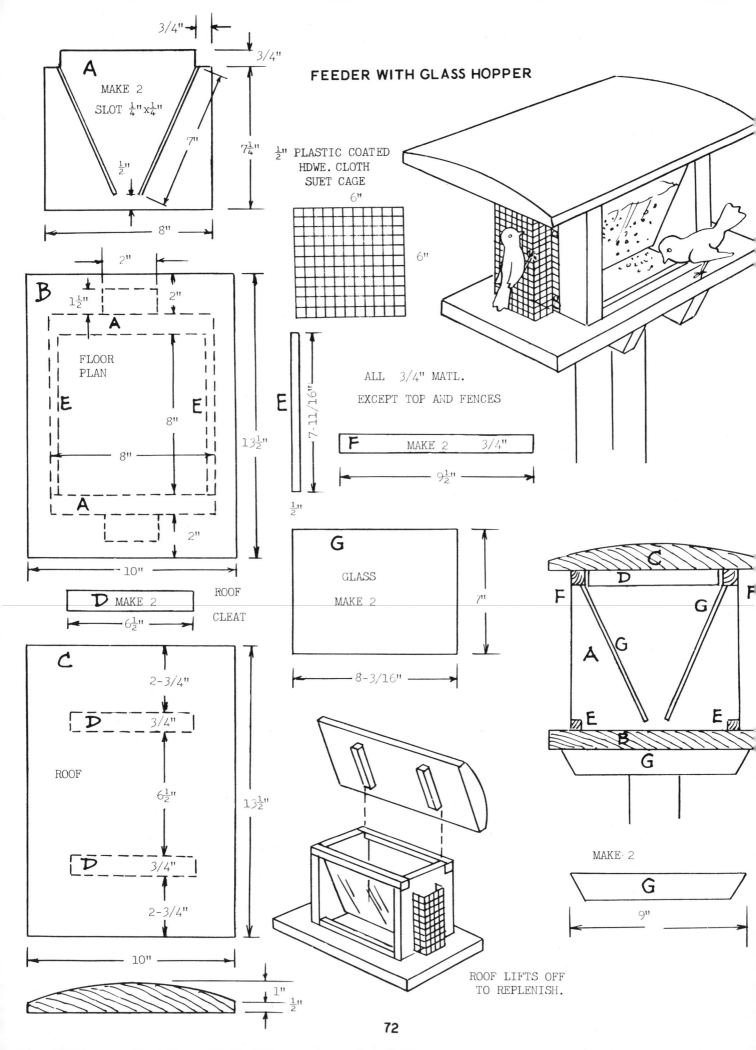

A
MAKE 2
SLOT ¼"x¼"

3/4"
3/4"
7"
7¼"
½"
8"

FEEDER WITH GLASS HOPPER

½" PLASTIC COATED
HDWE. CLOTH
SUET CAGE
6"
6"

B
FLOOR PLAN
2"
1½"
2"
A
E   E
8"
8"
A
2"
13½"
10"

E
7-11/16"
½"

ALL 3/4" MATL.
EXCEPT TOP AND FENCES

F   MAKE 2   3/4"
9½"

D MAKE 2   ROOF CLEAT
6½"

G
GLASS
MAKE 2
7"
8-3/16"

C
ROOF
2-3/4"
D   3/4"
6½"
D   3/4"
2-3/4"
13½"
10"

1"
½"

C
D
F   F
A   G   G
E   E
B
G

MAKE 2
G
9"

ROOF LIFTS OFF
TO REPLENISH.

72

CUPOLA FOR PURPLE MARTIN

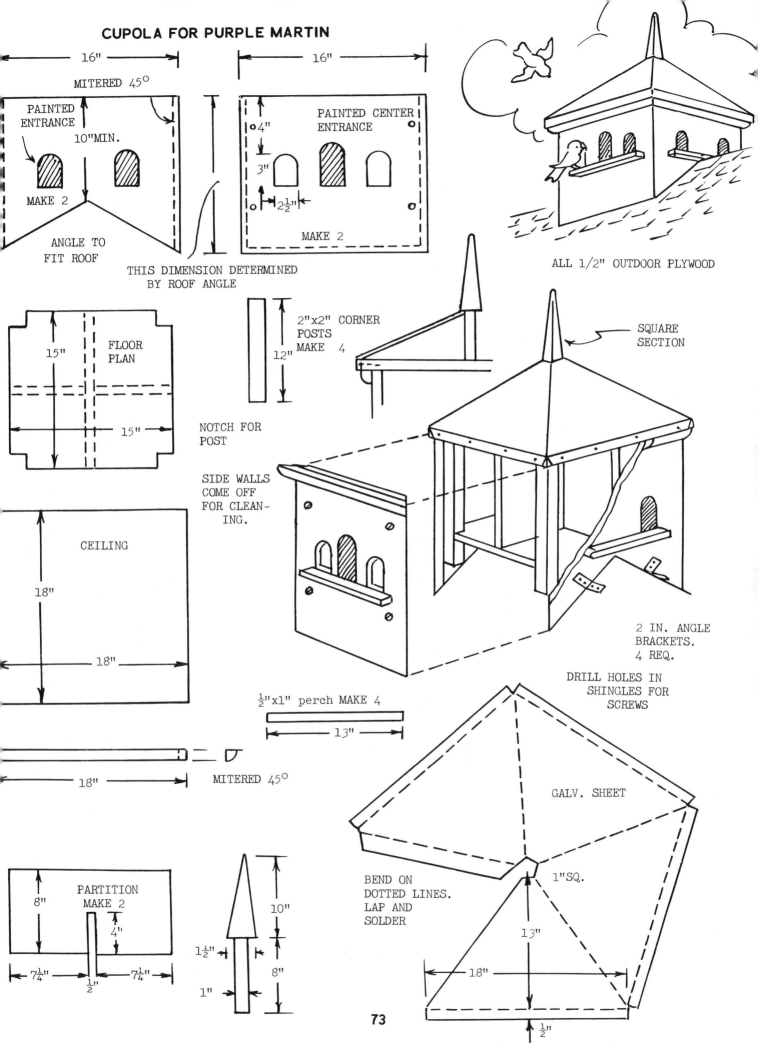

16"

MITERED 45°

PAINTED ENTRANCE

10" MIN.

MAKE 2

ANGLE TO FIT ROOF

16"

PAINTED CENTER ENTRANCE

4"

3"

2½"

MAKE 2

THIS DIMENSION DETERMINED BY ROOF ANGLE

ALL 1/2" OUTDOOR PLYWOOD

15"

FLOOR PLAN

15"

2"x2" CORNER POSTS MAKE 4

12"

NOTCH FOR POST

SQUARE SECTION

CEILING

18"

18"

SIDE WALLS COME OFF FOR CLEANING.

2 IN. ANGLE BRACKETS. 4 REQ.

DRILL HOLES IN SHINGLES FOR SCREWS

½"x1" perch MAKE 4

13"

18"

MITERED 45°

GALV. SHEET

PARTITION MAKE 2

8"

4"

7¼"

½"

7¼"

10"

8"

1½"

1"

BEND ON DOTTED LINES. LAP AND SOLDER

1"SQ.

13"

18"

½"

73

BIRD SANCTUARY

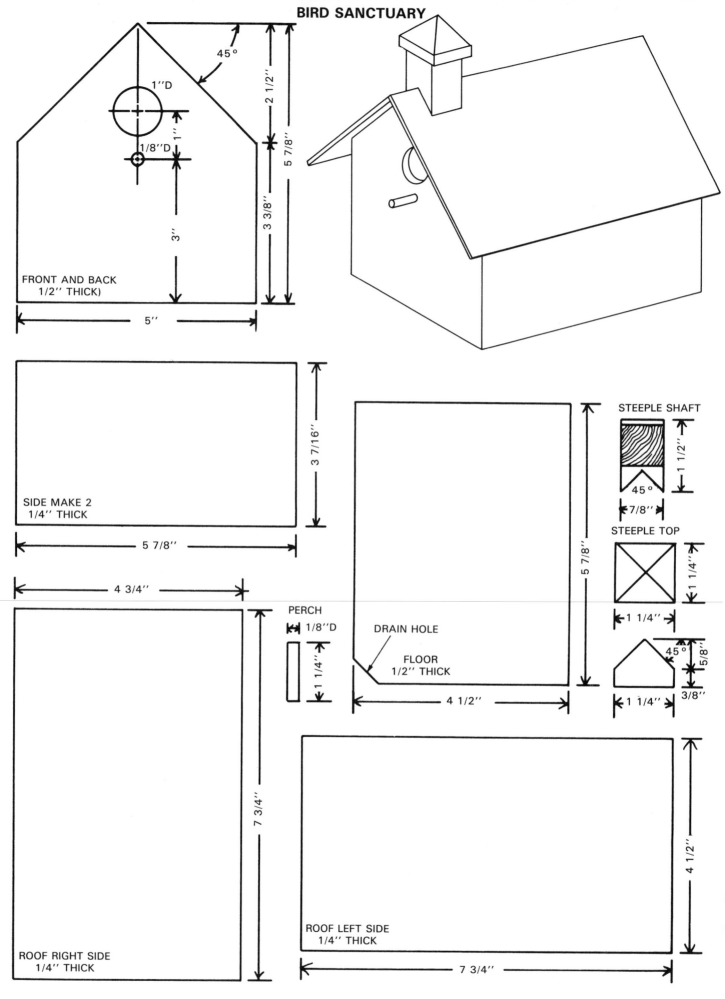

FRONT AND BACK
1/2'' THICK)

45°

1''D

1''

1/8''D

3''

3 3/8''

2 1/2''

5 7/8''

5''

SIDE MAKE 2
1/4'' THICK

3 7/16''

5 7/8''

4 3/4''

ROOF RIGHT SIDE
1/4'' THICK

7 3/4''

PERCH

1/8''D

1 1/4''

DRAIN HOLE

FLOOR
1/2'' THICK

4 1/2''

5 7/8''

STEEPLE SHAFT

1 1/2''

45°

7/8''

STEEPLE TOP

1 1/4''

1 1/4''

45°

5/8''

3/8''

1 1/4''

ROOF LEFT SIDE
1/4'' THICK

4 1/2''

7 3/4''

HOPPER FEEDER

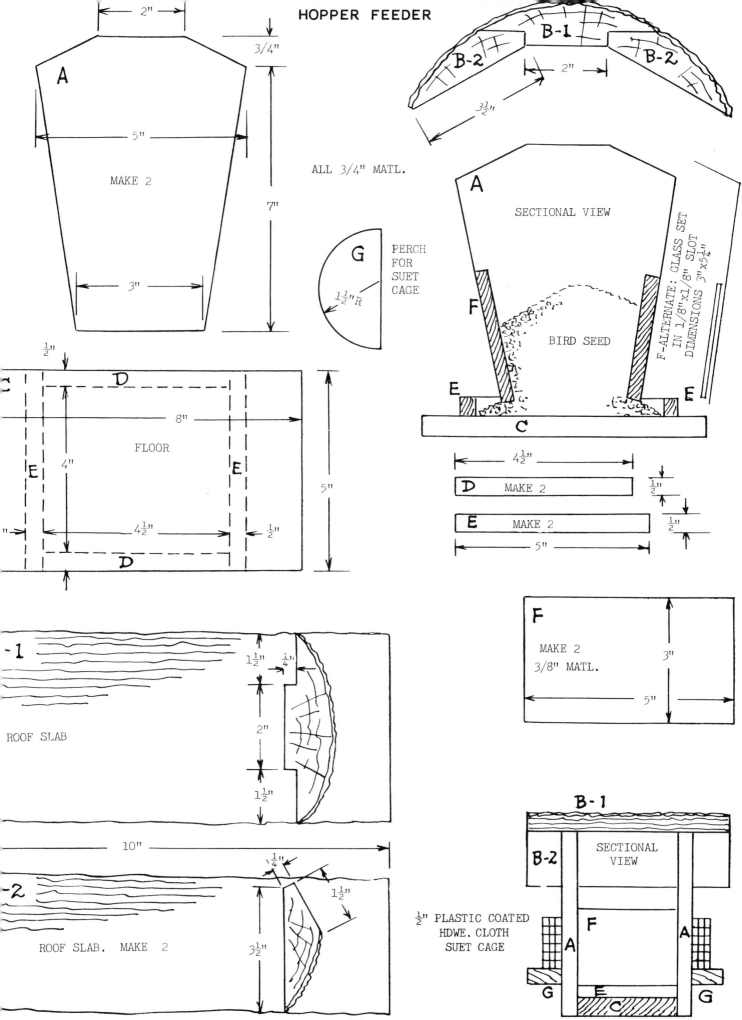

2"

3/4"

A

MAKE 2

5"

7"

3"

ALL 3/4" MATL.

G PERCH FOR SUET CAGE

1½"R

½"

D

FLOOR

8"

4"

E   E

4½"   ½"

5"

D

B-1

B-2   B-2

2"

3½"

A

SECTIONAL VIEW

F   F-ALTERNATE: GLASS SET IN 1/8"x1/8" SLOT DIMENSIONS 3"x5¼"

BIRD SEED

E   E

C

4½"

D   MAKE 2   ½"

E   MAKE 2   ½"

5"

F

MAKE 2
3/8" MATL.

3"

5"

-1

ROOF SLAB

1½"   ¼"

2"

1½"

10"

¼"

-2

ROOF SLAB. MAKE 2

1½"

3½"

B-1

B-2   SECTIONAL VIEW

½" PLASTIC COATED HDWE. CLOTH SUET CAGE

A   F   A

G   E   C   G

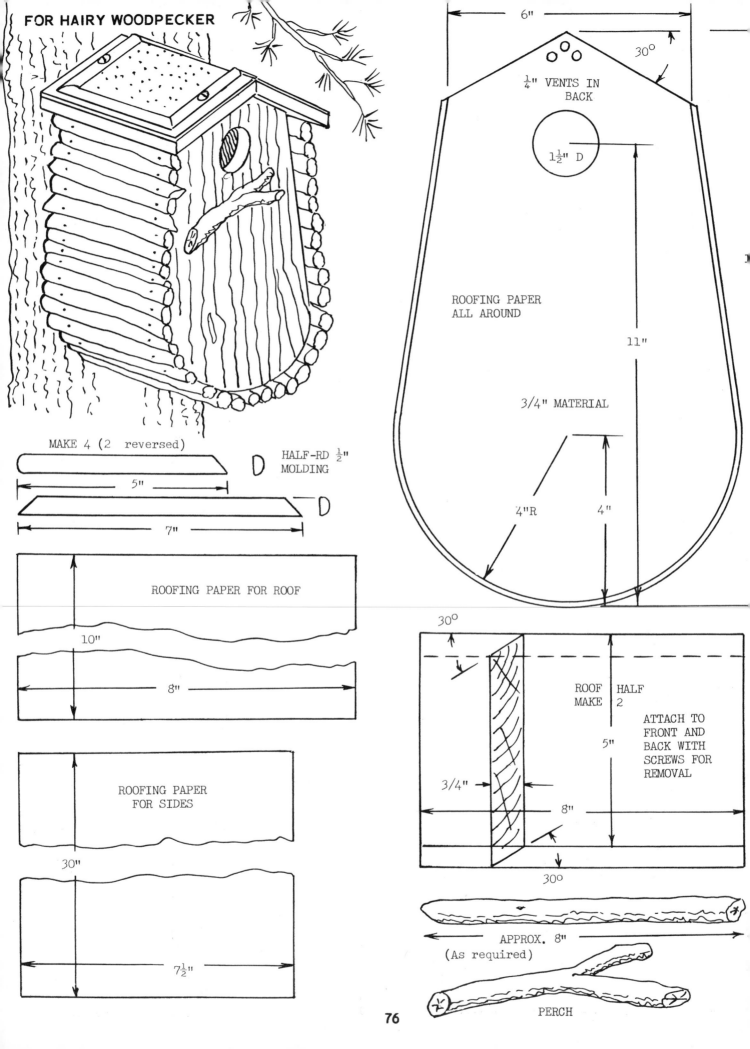

FOR HAIRY WOODPECKER

MAKE 4 (2 reversed)

HALF-RD ½"
MOLDING

D

5"

D

7"

ROOFING PAPER FOR ROOF

10"

8"

ROOFING PAPER
FOR SIDES

30"

7½"

6"

30°

¼" VENTS IN
BACK

1½" D

ROOFING PAPER
ALL AROUND

11"

3/4" MATERIAL

4"R

4"

30°

ROOF HALF
MAKE 2

ATTACH TO
FRONT AND
BACK WITH
SCREWS FOR
REMOVAL

5"

3/4"

8"

30°

APPROX. 8"
(As required)

PERCH

76

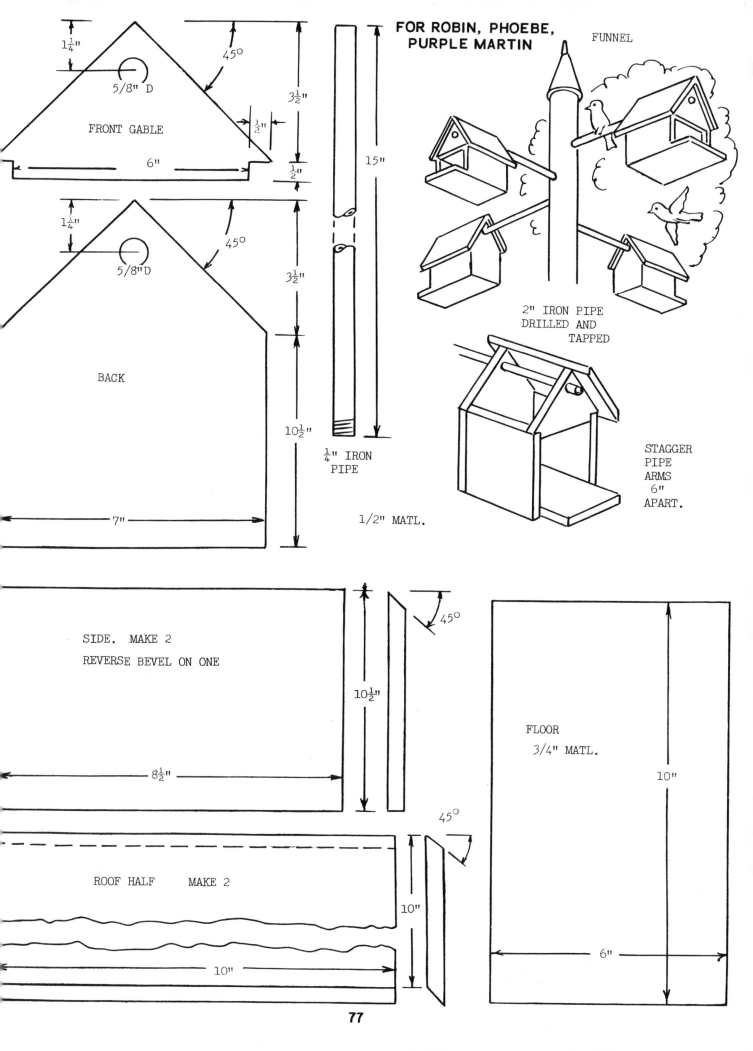

1¼"

5/8" D

FRONT GABLE

45°

3½"

½"

½"

6"

1¼"

5/8" D

45°

BACK

3½"

7"

10½"

15"

¼" IRON PIPE

1/2" MATL.

FOR ROBIN, PHOEBE, PURPLE MARTIN

FUNNEL

2" IRON PIPE DRILLED AND TAPPED

STAGGER PIPE ARMS 6" APART.

SIDE. MAKE 2
REVERSE BEVEL ON ONE

45°

10½"

8½"

45°

ROOF HALF   MAKE 2

10"

10"

FLOOR
3/4" MATL.

10"

6"

77

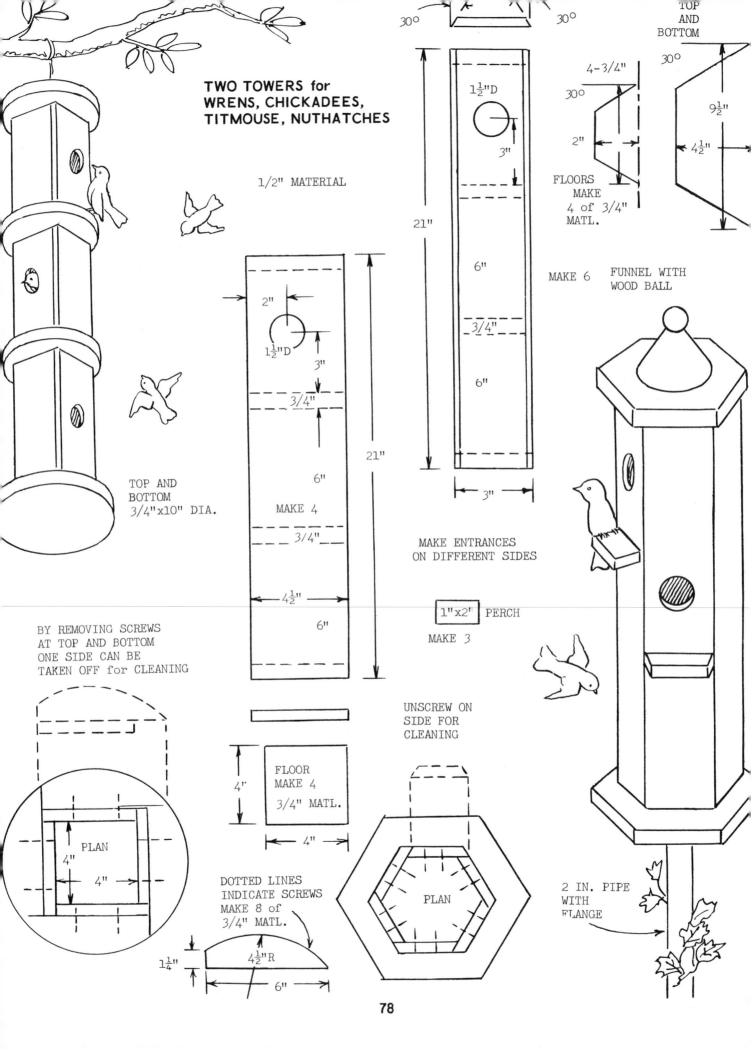

TWO TOWERS for WRENS, CHICKADEES, TITMOUSE, NUTHATCHES

1/2" MATERIAL

TOP AND BOTTOM
3/4"x10" DIA.

2"

1½"D

3"

3/4"

6"

21"

3/4"

6"

4½"

6"

MAKE 4

BY REMOVING SCREWS
AT TOP AND BOTTOM
ONE SIDE CAN BE
TAKEN OFF for CLEANING

PLAN

4"

4"

DOTTED LINES
INDICATE SCREWS
MAKE 8 of
3/4" MATL.

1¼"

4½"R

6"

30°

30°

30°

1½"D

3"

21"

6"

3/4"

6"

3"

MAKE ENTRANCES
ON DIFFERENT SIDES

1"x2" PERCH

MAKE 3

UNSCREW ON
SIDE FOR
CLEANING

FLOOR
MAKE 4
3/4" MATL.

4"

4"

PLAN

TOP AND BOTTOM

4-3/4"

30°

2"

9½"

4½"

FLOORS
MAKE
4 of 3/4"
MATL.

MAKE 6   FUNNEL WITH
WOOD BALL

2 IN. PIPE
WITH
FLANGE

78

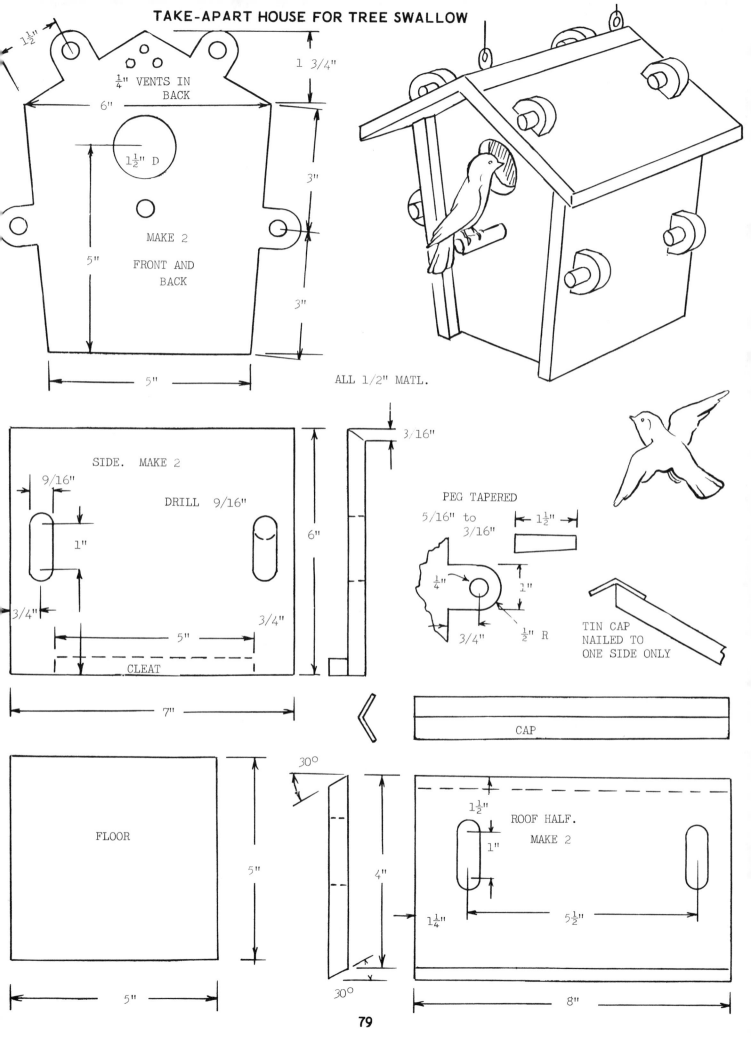

1½"

¼" VENTS IN
BACK

6"

1½" D

1 3/4"

3"

MAKE 2

FRONT AND
BACK

5"

3"

5"

ALL 1/2" MATL.

SIDE. MAKE 2

DRILL 9/16"

9/16"

1"

6"

3/16"

3/4"

3/4"

5"

CLEAT

7"

PEG TAPERED

5/16" to
3/16"

1½"

¼"

1"

3/4"

½" R

TIN CAP
NAILED TO
ONE SIDE ONLY

CAP

FLOOR

5"

5"

30°

4"

30°

1½"

ROOF HALF.

MAKE 2

1"

1¼"

5½"

8"

FUNNEL FEEDER

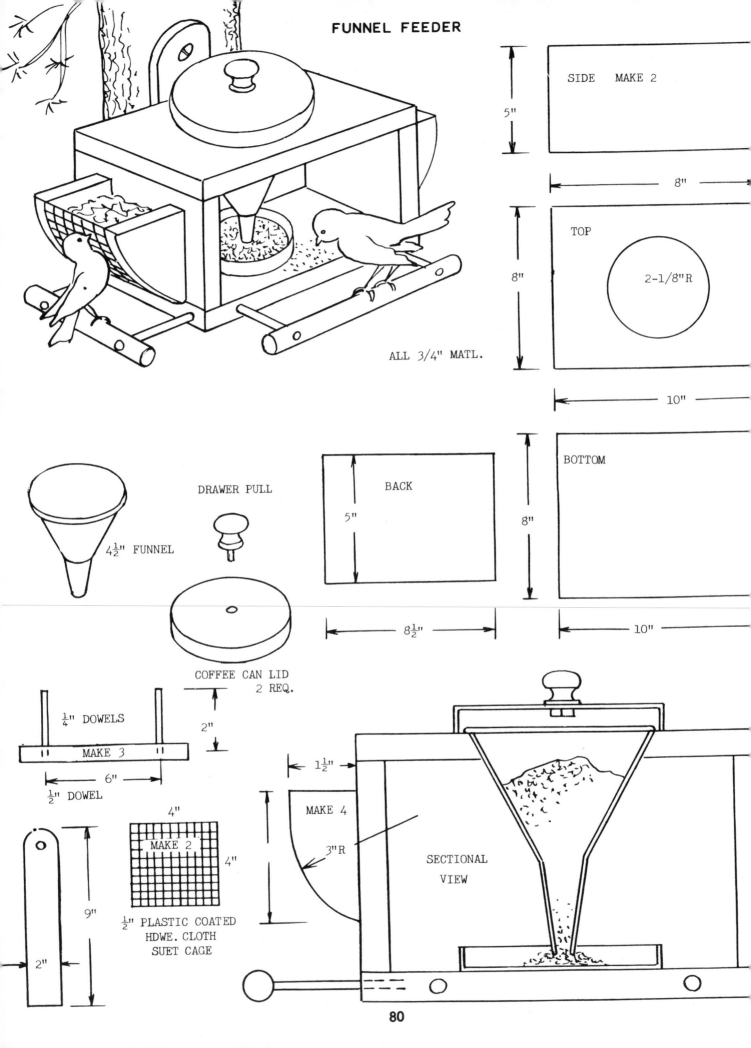

SIDE   MAKE 2

5"

8"

TOP

8"

2-1/8"R

10"

BACK

5"

BOTTOM

8"

8½"

10"

4½" FUNNEL

DRAWER PULL

COFFEE CAN LID
2 REQ.

ALL 3/4" MATL.

¼" DOWELS

MAKE 3

2"

6"

½" DOWEL

4"

MAKE 2

4"

½" PLASTIC COATED
HDWE. CLOTH
SUET CAGE

9"

2"

1½"

MAKE 4

3"R

SECTIONAL
VIEW

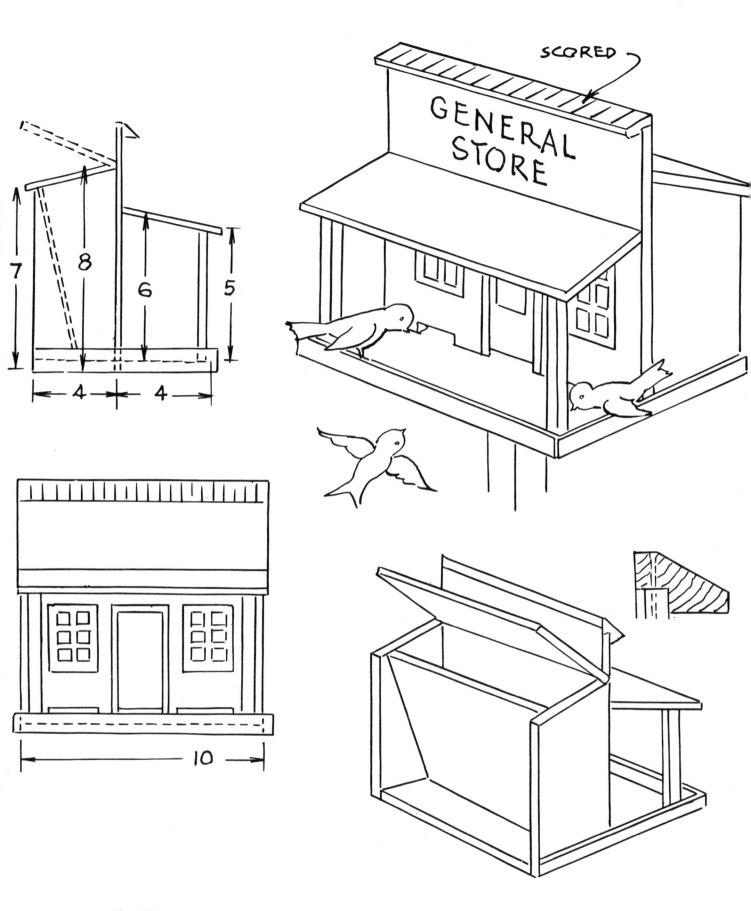

SCORED

GENERAL
STORE

7 8 6 5

4 4

10

The GENERAL STORE has 3/8 slots under dummy windows and door for the bird seed to spill out. Lid over hopper is hinged for filling.
WINDOW FEEDER below may be made full width of window, or smaller with shut-off panels to enclose open space. It screws to sill, with a tapered filler being used to bring it level. Window Sash is raised for replenishing. Use 3/4 in. material, with 3/8 dowel perch.

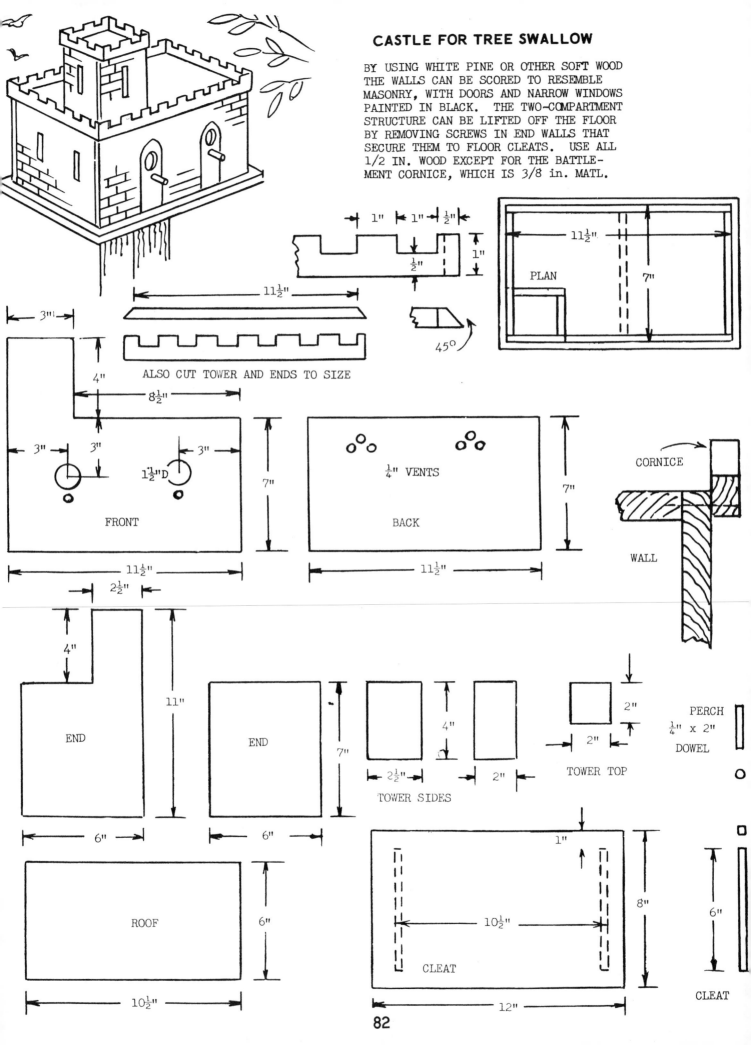

CASTLE FOR TREE SWALLOW

BY USING WHITE PINE OR OTHER SOFT WOOD
THE WALLS CAN BE SCORED TO RESEMBLE
MASONRY, WITH DOORS AND NARROW WINDOWS
PAINTED IN BLACK. THE TWO-COMPARTMENT
STRUCTURE CAN BE LIFTED OFF THE FLOOR
BY REMOVING SCREWS IN END WALLS THAT
SECURE THEM TO FLOOR CLEATS. USE ALL
1/2 IN. WOOD EXCEPT FOR THE BATTLE-
MENT CORNICE, WHICH IS 3/8 in. MATL.

PLAN

ALSO CUT TOWER AND ENDS TO SIZE

FRONT

BACK

¼" VENTS

CORNICE

WALL

END

END

TOWER SIDES

TOWER TOP

PERCH
¼" x 2"
DOWEL

ROOF

CLEAT

CLEAT

82

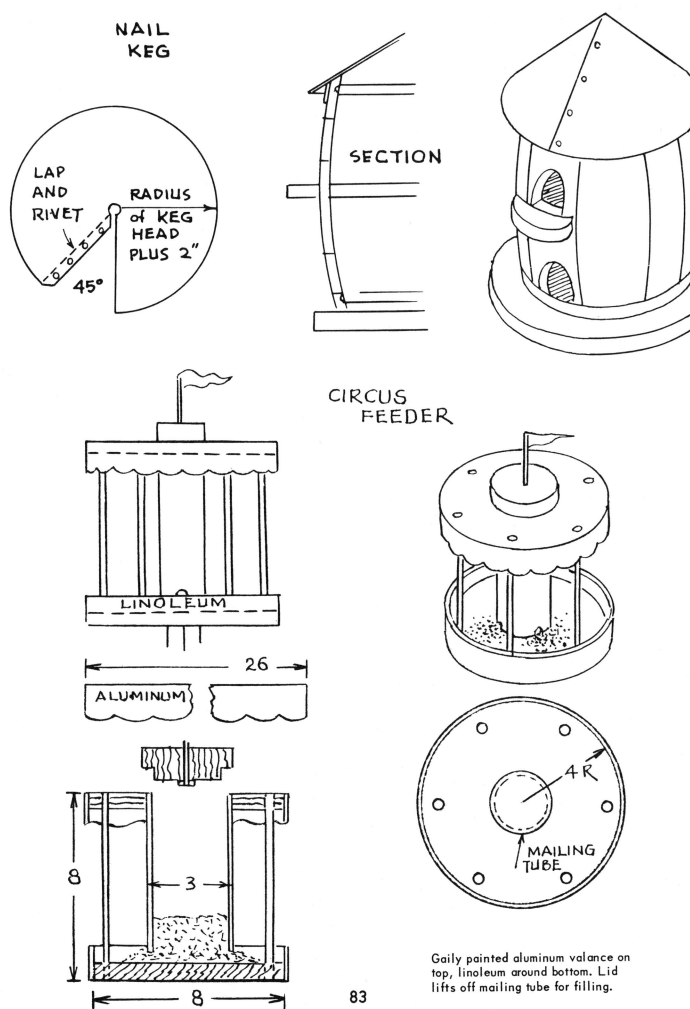

NAIL
KEG

LAP
AND
RIVET

RADIUS
of KEG
HEAD
PLUS 2"

45°

SECTION

CIRCUS
FEEDER

LINOLEUM

26

ALUMINUM

8

3

8

4 R

MAILING
TUBE

Gaily painted aluminum valance on
top, linoleum around bottom. Lid
lifts off mailing tube for filling.

83

TWIN SEED DISPENSER

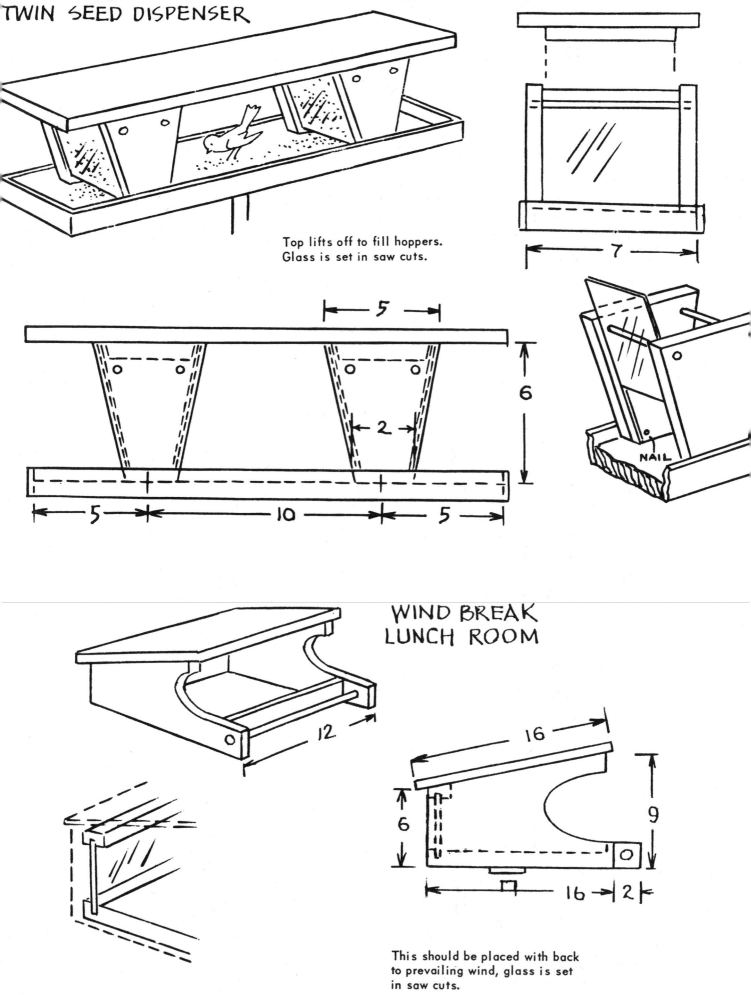

Top lifts off to fill hoppers.
Glass is set in saw cuts.

7

5

6

2

5   10   5

NAIL

WIND BREAK
LUNCH ROOM

12

16

6

9

16   2

This should be placed with back
to prevailing wind, glass is set
in saw cuts.

84

COAXER FEEDER

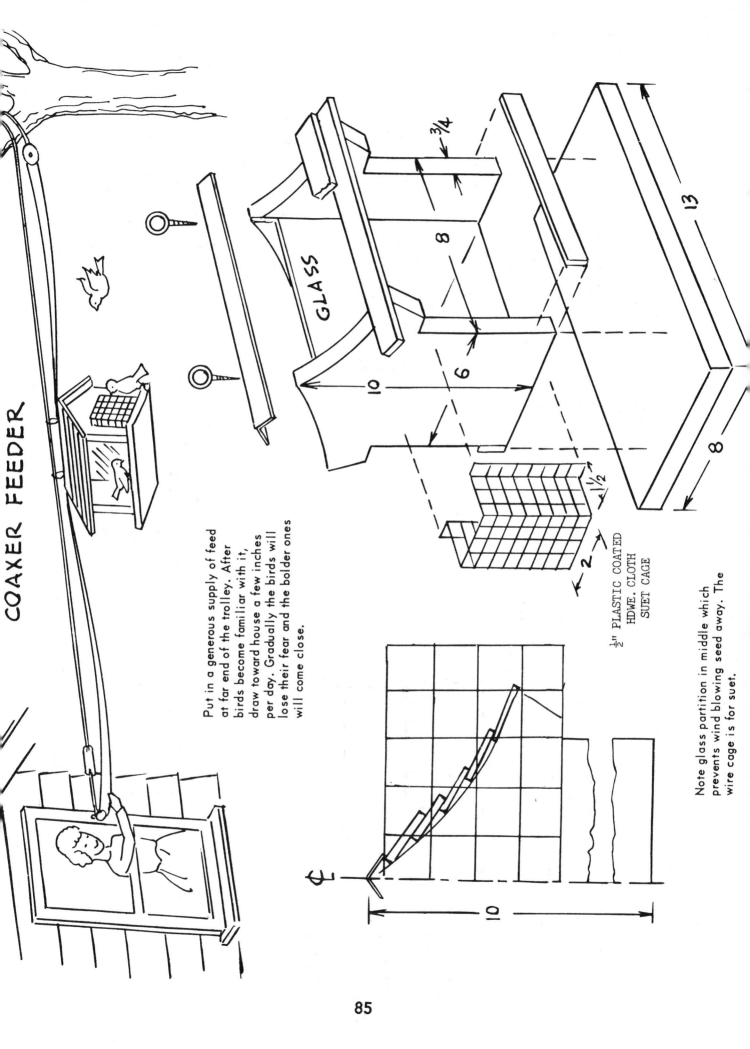

Put in a generous supply of feed at far end of the trolley. After birds become familiar with it, draw toward house a few inches per day. Gradually the birds will lose their fear and the bolder ones will come close.

GLASS

3/4

8

6

10

13

8

1/2

2

$\frac{1}{2}$" PLASTIC COATED HDWE. CLOTH SUET CAGE

10

Note glass partition in middle which prevents wind blowing seed away. The wire cage is for suet.

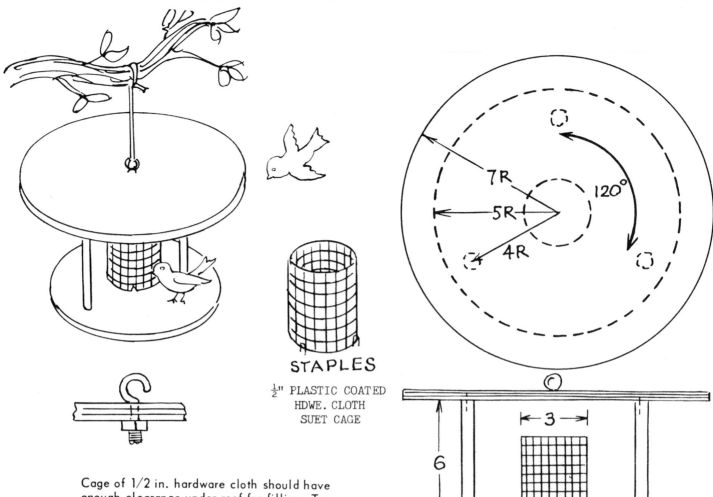

STAPLES

½" PLASTIC COATED
HDWE. CLOTH
SUET CAGE

Cage of 1/2 in. hardware cloth should have
enough clearance under roof for filling. Top
and bottom are joined with three 1/2 in.
dowels.

7R

5R

4R

120°

6

3

JIFFY JOB

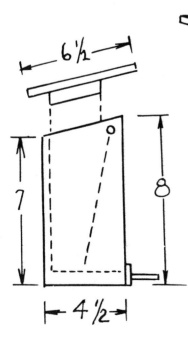

6½

7

4½

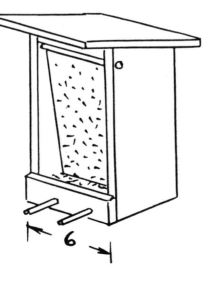

6

A "jiffy" feeder that can be
whipped up in one evening.
As sides must be slotted for
the glass hopper they should
be at least 1/2 in. stock.

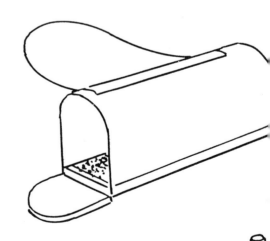

Weld sheet metal vane
to top of mail box. Mount
on ball bearing.

GLASS IN SLOT

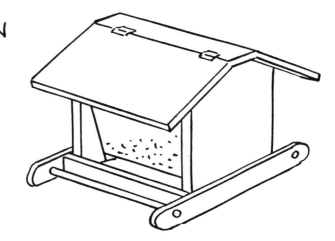

Another type glass hopper, with one half of lid hinged for filling.

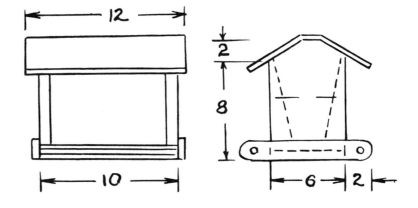

12

10

2

8

6 2

FOR A WALL

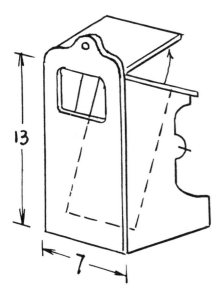

13

7

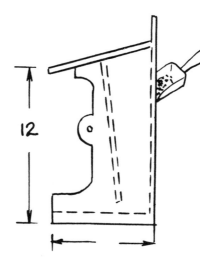

12

Hopper type with opening in back to put in seed. Suet filled cage is held in place with rod.

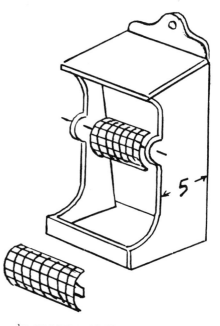

5

$\frac{1}{2}$" PLASTIC COATED
HDWE. CLOTH
SUET CAGE

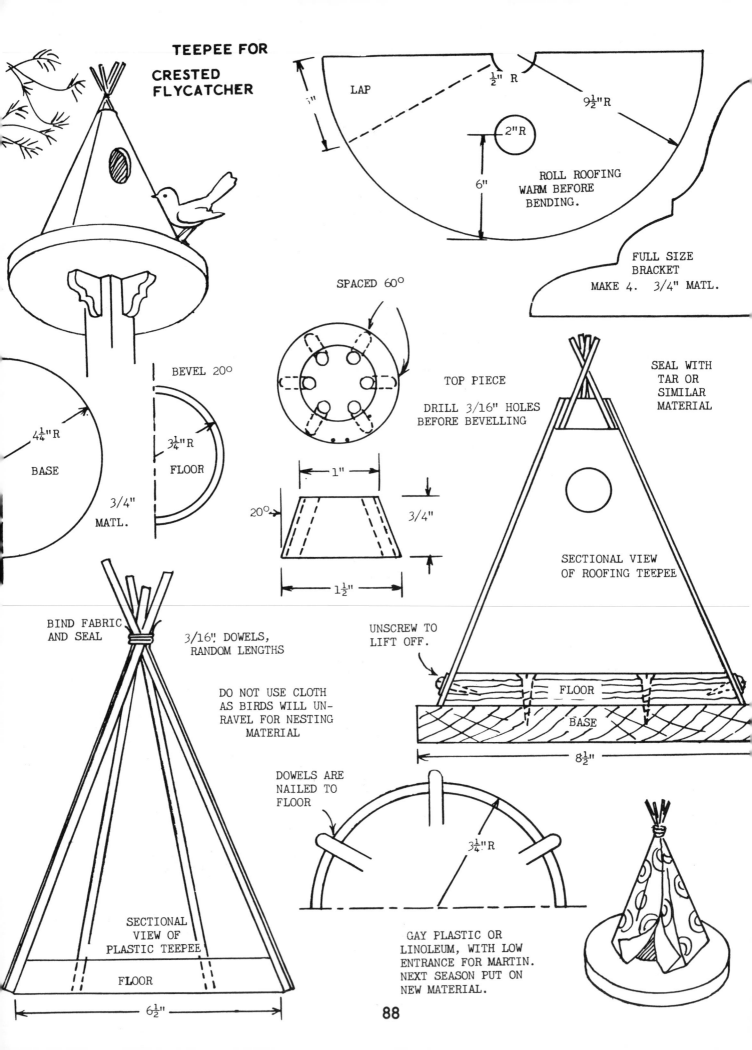

TEEPEE FOR
CRESTED FLYCATCHER

LAP

½" R

9½"R

2"R

6"

ROLL ROOFING
WARM BEFORE
BENDING.

FULL SIZE
BRACKET
MAKE 4. 3/4" MATL.

SPACED 60°

TOP PIECE

DRILL 3/16" HOLES
BEFORE BEVELLING

BEVEL 20°

4¼"R

BASE

3/4"
MATL.

3½"R

FLOOR

1"

20°

3/4"

1½"

SEAL WITH
TAR OR
SIMILAR
MATERIAL

SECTIONAL VIEW
OF ROOFING TEEPEE

BIND FABRIC
AND SEAL

3/16" DOWELS,
RANDOM LENGTHS

DO NOT USE CLOTH
AS BIRDS WILL UN-
RAVEL FOR NESTING
MATERIAL

UNSCREW TO
LIFT OFF.

FLOOR

BASE

8½"

DOWELS ARE
NAILED TO
FLOOR

3½"R

SECTIONAL
VIEW OF
PLASTIC TEEPEE

FLOOR

6½"

GAY PLASTIC OR
LINOLEUM, WITH LOW
ENTRANCE FOR MARTIN.
NEXT SEASON PUT ON
NEW MATERIAL.

VANE CAFE

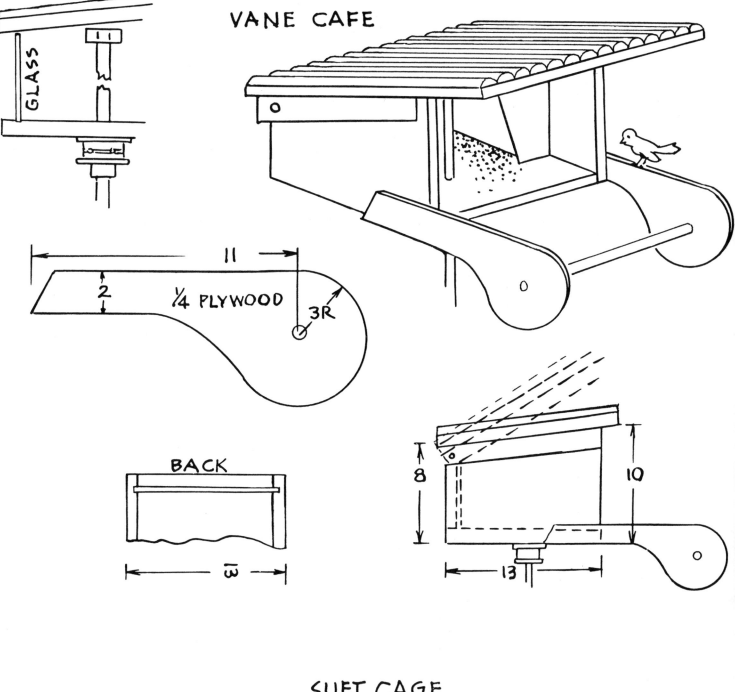

GLASS

11

2

¼ PLYWOOD

3R

BACK

13

8

10

13

SUET CAGE

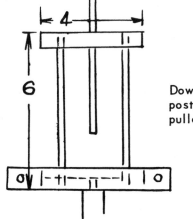

4

6

Dowel suet cage for
post. One dowel is
pulled up for filling.

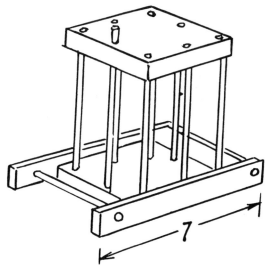

7

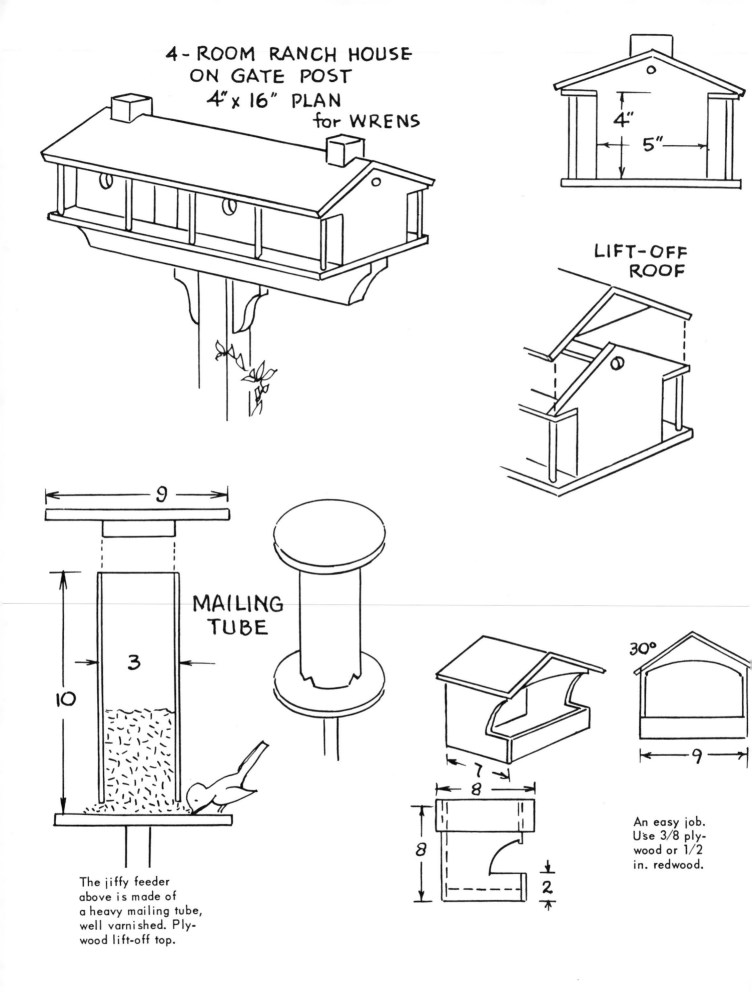

4-ROOM RANCH HOUSE
ON GATE POST
4"x 16" PLAN
for WRENS

4"

5"

LIFT-OFF
ROOF

9

MAILING
TUBE

10

3

The jiffy feeder
above is made of
a heavy mailing tube,
well varnished. Ply-
wood lift-off top.

7

8

8

2

30°

9

An easy job.
Use 3/8 ply-
wood or 1/2
in. redwood.

90

SWIVEL TOP CAFE

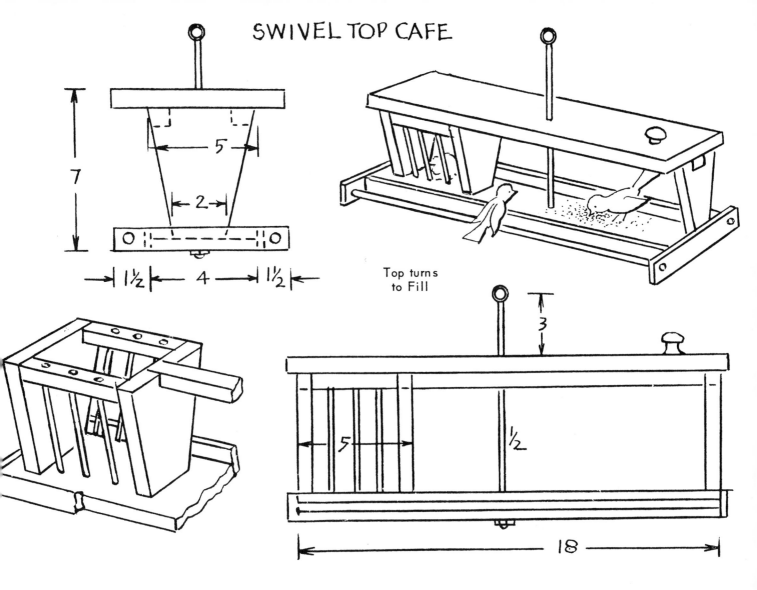

7

5

2

1½ 4 1½

Top turns
to Fill

3

5 ½

18

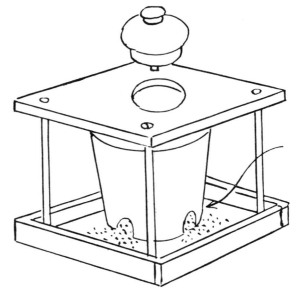

Teakettle lid

6

8

Make three 1/2 in.
holes in flower pot

ORIENTAL CAFE

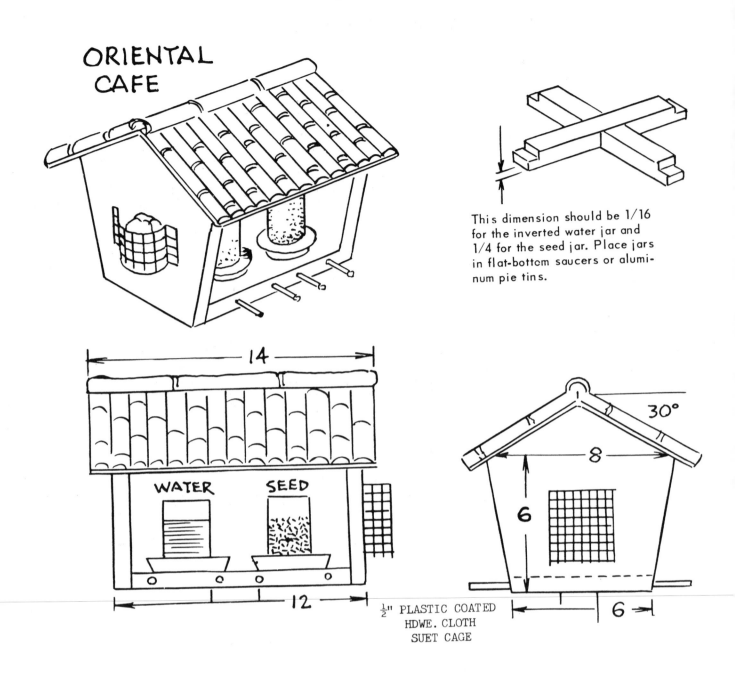

This dimension should be 1/16 for the inverted water jar and 1/4 for the seed jar. Place jars in flat-bottom saucers or aluminum pie tins.

14

WATER   SEED

12

30°

8

6

6

½" PLASTIC COATED HDWE. CLOTH SUET CAGE

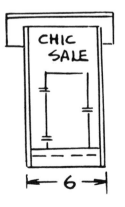

CHIC SALE

6

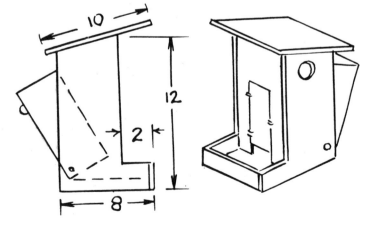

10

12

2

8

This "Old Timer" has a hinged tin hopper opening from the back. Door is a painted dummy.

WINDOW FEEDER

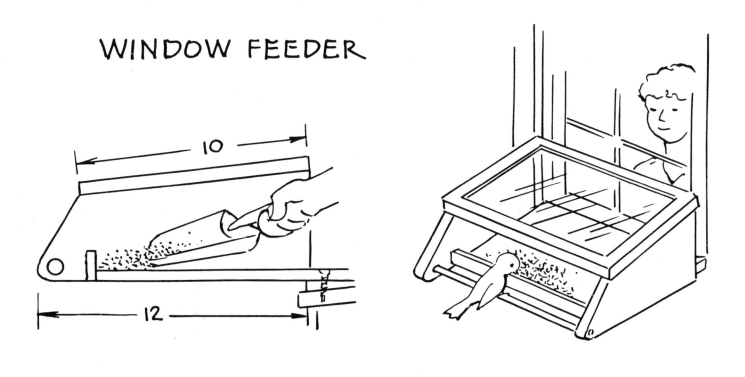

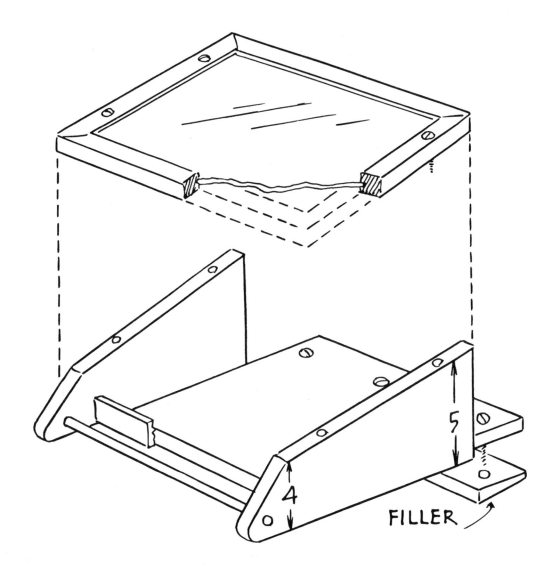

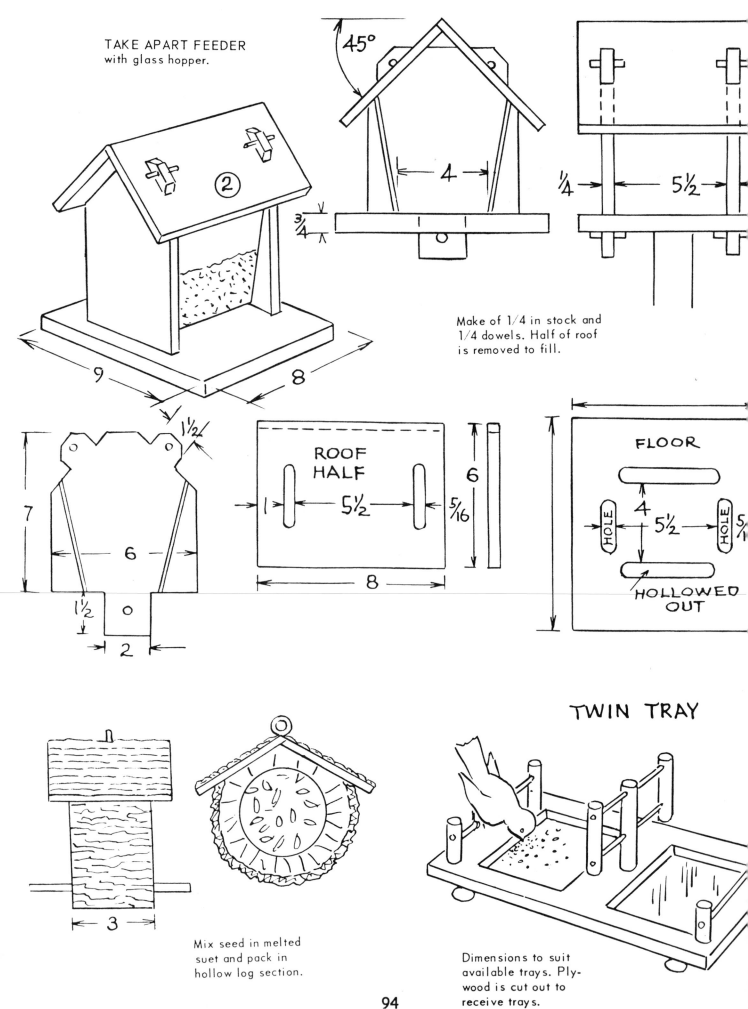

TAKE APART FEEDER
with glass hopper.

45°

4

3/4

Make of 1/4 in stock and
1/4 dowels. Half of roof
is removed to fill.

1/4   5½

②

9   8

1½

7

6

1½

2

ROOF
HALF

1   5½   5/16

6

8

FLOOR

HOLE   4   5½   HOLE

HOLLOWED
OUT

3

Mix seed in melted
suet and pack in
hollow log section.

TWIN TRAY

Dimensions to suit
available trays. Ply-
wood is cut out to
receive trays.

94

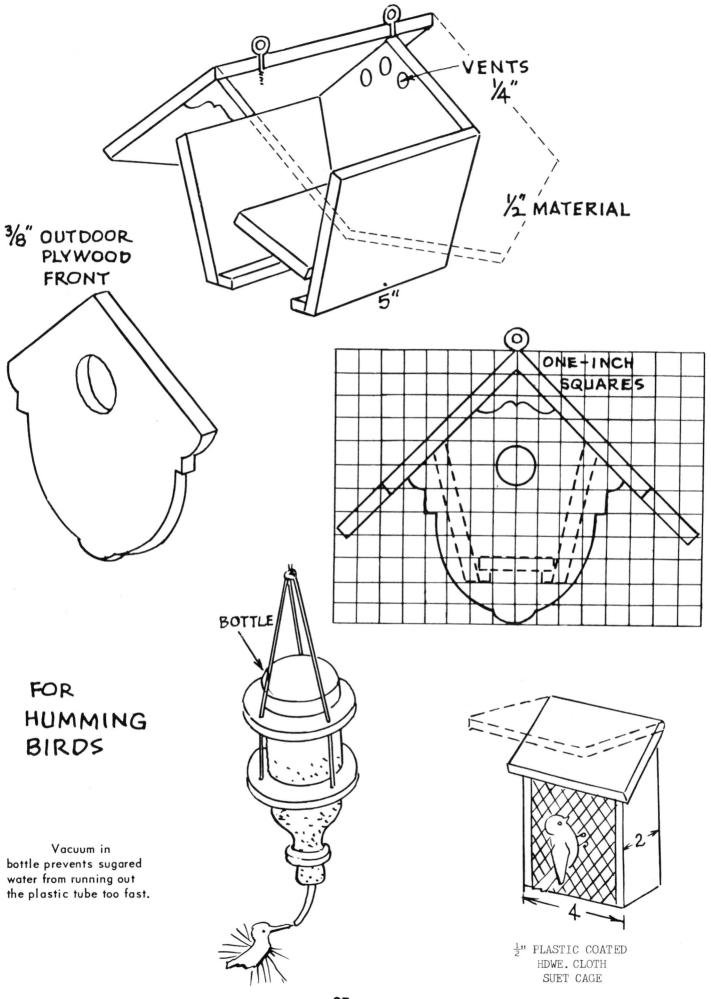

VENTS
¼"

½" MATERIAL

5"

⅜" OUTDOOR
PLYWOOD
FRONT

ONE-INCH
SQUARES

BOTTLE

FOR
HUMMING
BIRDS

Vacuum in
bottle prevents sugared
water from running out
the plastic tube too fast.

2

4

½" PLASTIC COATED
HDWE. CLOTH
SUET CAGE

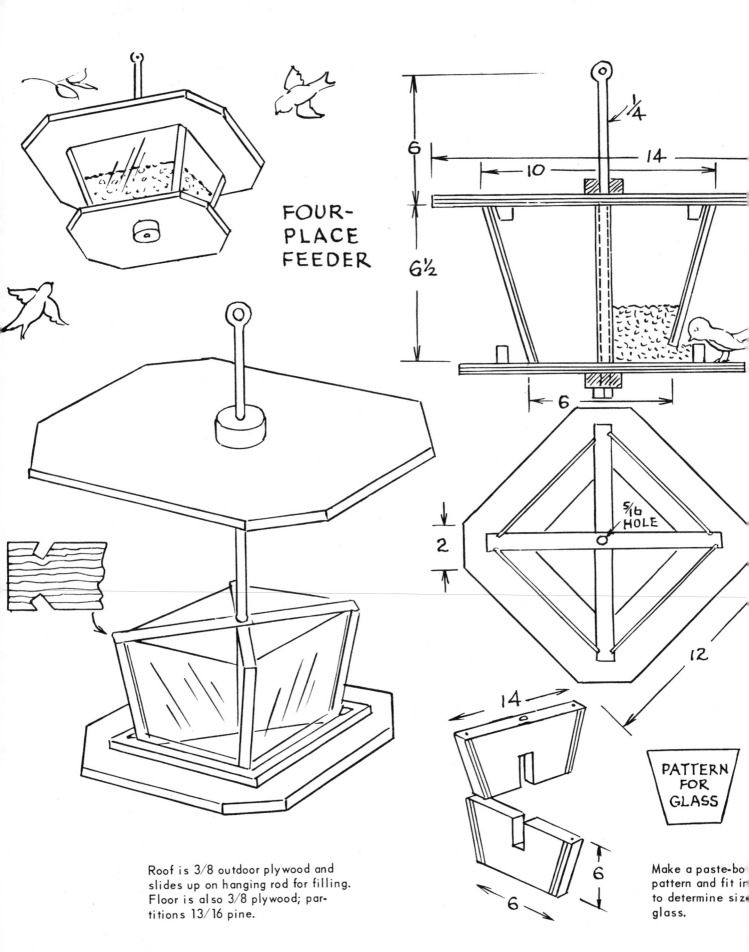

FOUR-
PLACE
FEEDER

6

6½

¼

10

14

6

5/16
HOLE

2

12

14

6

6

PATTERN
FOR
GLASS

Roof is 3/8 outdoor plywood and slides up on hanging rod for filling. Floor is also 3/8 plywood; partitions 13/16 pine.

Make a paste-bo
pattern and fit in
to determine size
glass.